Teach Yourself VISUALLY™

Windows® 10

Paul McFedries

Visual
A Wiley Brand

Teach Yourself VISUALLY™ Windows® 10

Published by
John Wiley & Sons, Inc.
10475 Crosspoint Boulevard
Indianapolis, IN 46256

www.wiley.com

Published simultaneously in Canada

Wiley publishes in a variety of print and electronic formats and by print-on-demand. Some material included with standard print versions of this book may not be included in e-books or in print-on-demand. If this book refers to media such as a CD or DVD that is not included in the version you purchased, you may download this material at http://booksupport.wiley.com. For more information about Wiley products, visit www.wiley.com.

Library of Congress Control Number: 2015945792

ISBN: 978-1-119-05702-4 (pbk); ISBN: 978-1-119-05704-8 (ebk); ISBN: 978-1-119-05716-1 (ebk)

Manufactured in the United States of America

10 9 8 7 6 5 4 3 2 1

Trademark Acknowledgments

Contact Us

For general information on our other products and services please contact our Customer Care Department within the U.S. at 877-762-2974, outside the U.S. at 317-572-3993 or fax 317-572-4002.

For technical support please visit www.wiley.com/techsupport.

Credits

Acquisitions Editor
Aaron Black

Project Editor
Sarah Hellert

Technical Editor
Vince Averello

Copy Editor
Scott Tullis

Production Editor
Barath Kumar Rajasekaran

Manager, Content Development & Assembly
Mary Beth Wakefield

Vice President, Professional Technology Strategy
Barry Pruett

About the Author

Paul McFedries is a full-time technical writer. Paul has been authoring computer books since 1991, and he has more than 85 books to his credit. Paul's books have sold more than four million copies worldwide. These books include the Wiley titles *Teach Yourself VISUALLY OS X Yosemite*, *The Facebook Guide for People Over 50*, *iPhone 6 Portable Genius*, and *iPad Portable Genius*, 3rd Edition. Paul is also the proprietor of Word Spy (www.wordspy.com), a website that tracks new words and phrases as they enter the language. Paul invites you to drop by his personal website at www.mcfedries.com or follow him on Twitter @wordspy.

Author's Acknowledgments

It goes without saying that writers focus on text, and I certainly enjoyed focusing on the text that you'll read in this book. However, this book is more than just the usual collection of words and phrases. A quick thumb through the pages will show you that this book is also chock-full of images, from sharp screen shots to fun and informative illustrations. Those colorful images sure make for a beautiful book, and that beauty comes from a lot of hard work by Wiley's immensely talented group of designers and layout artists. I thank them for creating another gem. Of course, what you read in this book must also be accurate, logically presented, and free of errors. Ensuring all of this was an excellent group of editors that included project editor Sarah Hellert, copy editor Scott Tullis, and technical editor Vince Averello. Thanks to all of you for your exceptional competence and hard work. Thanks, as well, to Wiley acquisitions editor Aaron Black for asking me to write this book.

How to Use This Book

Who This Book Is For

This book is for the reader who has never used this particular technology or software application. It is also for readers who want to expand their knowledge.

The Conventions in This Book

❶ Steps

This book uses a step-by-step format to guide you easily through each task. Numbered steps are actions you must do; bulleted steps clarify a point, step, or optional feature; and indented steps give you the result.

❷ Notes

Notes give additional information — special conditions that may occur during an operation, a situation that you want to avoid, or a cross reference to a related area of the book.

❸ Icons and Buttons

Icons and buttons show you exactly what you need to click to perform a step.

❹ Tips

Tips offer additional information, including warnings and shortcuts.

❺ Bold

Bold type shows command names, options, and text or numbers you must type.

❻ Italics

Italic type introduces and defines a new term.

Table of Contents

Chapter 3 Surfing the Web

"Observations of a "Webliographer," *Information Outlook*,

Great word! Do you have this one in the Word Spy database?

hich links on a Web page become obsolete as the sites

to change location or die.

, "Jargon Watch," *Wired*, July 1, 1996

Fun column!

Chapter 4 Sending and Receiving Email

Choose an account

Outlook.com
Outlook.com, Live.com, Hotmail, MSN

Exchange
Exchange, Office 365

Google

Yahoo! Mail

iCloud

Other account
POP, IMAP

Table of Contents

Chapter 7 Working with Images

Table of Contents

Chapter 8 — Working with Multimedia

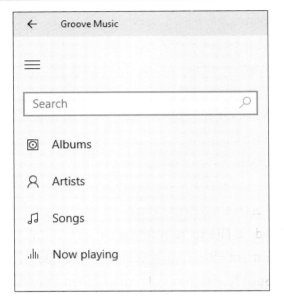

Chapter 9 — Editing Documents

Chapter 10 Working with Files

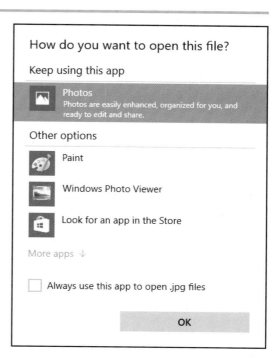

Chapter 11 Sharing Your Computer

Table of Contents

Chapter 12 Getting More from a Tablet PC

Chapter 13 Implementing Security

Getting Started with Windows

To do something useful with your computer and with Windows 10, you need to explore the screen, connect to your network, and learn how to work with apps.

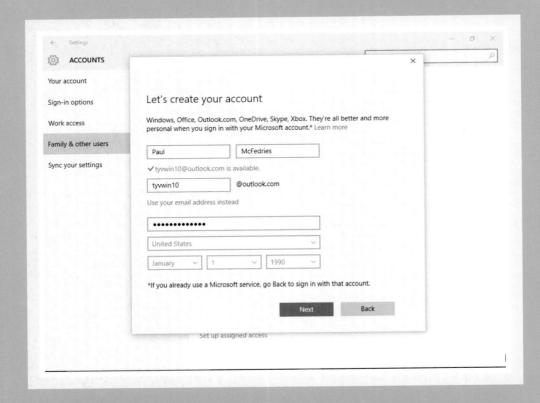

Explore the PC Screen

Before getting to the specifics of working with Windows 10, take a few seconds to familiarize yourself with the basic elements of the screen. These elements include the Start screen's app tiles, live tiles, your user tile, and the Desktop tile.

Understanding where these elements appear on the Start screen and what they are used for will help you work through the rest of this book and will help you navigate Windows and its applications on your own. This section covers the screen you see on a PC. If you are using a Touch PC or a tablet, see the next section, "Explore the Tablet Screen."

A Desktop Icon

An icon on the desktop represents a program or Windows feature. A program you install often adds its own icon on the desktop.

B Mouse Pointer

When you move your mouse, this pointer moves along with it.

C Desktop

This is the Windows "work area," meaning that it is where you work with your programs and documents.

D Start Button

You use this button to start programs and launch many of Windows' features.

E Search Box

You use this box to search for items on your PC or on the Internet.

F Taskbar Icons

You use these icons to launch some Windows features with just a mouse click.

G Taskbar

The programs you have open appear in the taskbar. You use this area to switch between programs if you have more than one running at a time.

H Notification Area

This area displays small icons that notify you about things that are happening on your computer. For example, you see notifications if your printer runs out of paper or if an update to Windows is available over the Internet.

I Time and Date

This is the current time and date on your computer. To see the full date, position the mouse () over the time. To change the date or time, click the time.

Explore the Tablet Screen

If you are using a touch-based PC or a tablet device, Windows 10 will automatically reconfigure the screen into *tablet mode,* which is designed to make it easier for you to navigate and launch items using touches and other gestures. However, you might find that using this new interface is not easier at first. To get more out of this interface and to learn how to operate your Touch PC or tablet, you need to familiarize yourself with Windows 10's tablet mode.

Explore the Tablet Screen

Ⓐ Tablet mode displays the Start screen, which consists of *tiles* for several common apps.

Ⓑ In an app, you can click **Back** (⬅) to return to either the previous app screen or to the Start screen.

Ⓒ To return directly to the Start screen, you can click **Start** (⊞).

① To see more commands, click **Menu** (≡).

Windows displays a menu of commands.

② To hide the commands, click **Menu** (≡) again.

Ⓓ To toggle tablet mode on and off, you can click **Action Center** (🗔) and then click **Tablet Mode**.

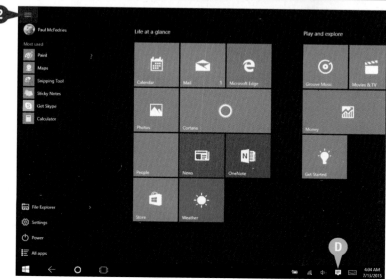

5

Put Windows to Sleep

You can make your computer more energy efficient by putting Windows into sleep mode when you are not using the computer. *Sleep mode* means that your computer is in a temporary low-power mode. This saves electricity when your computer is plugged in, and it saves battery power when your computer is unplugged.

In sleep mode, Windows keeps your apps open. This is handy because it means that when you return from sleep mode, after you sign in to Windows again, you can immediately get back to what you were doing.

Put Windows to Sleep

1 Click **Start** (⊞).

The Start menu appears.

2 Click **Power** (⏻).

3 Click **Sleep**.

Windows activates sleep mode.

Note: To return from sleep mode, press your computer's Power button.

Restart or Shut Down Windows

You can restart Windows, which means that it shuts down and starts up again immediately. This is useful if your computer is running slowly or acting funny. Sometimes a restart solves the problem.

Alternatively, when you complete your work, you could shut down Windows. However, do not just shut off your computer's power because doing so can cause problems: If you have documents with unsaved changes, you may lose those changes; you also could damage one or more Windows system files, which could make your system unstable. Therefore, you should always follow the proper steps when shutting down your PC.

Restart or Shut Down Windows

1 Shut down all your running programs.

Note: Be sure to save your work as you close your programs.

2 Click **Start** (⊞).

The Start menu appears.

3 Click **Power** (⏻).

4 Click a command:

Ⓐ Click **Restart** to shut down and then start your computer.

Ⓑ Click **Shut Down** to turn off your computer.

Connect to Your Wireless Network

If you have a wireless access point and your computer has built-in wireless networking capabilities, you can connect to the wireless access point to access your network. If your wireless access point is connected to the Internet, then connecting to the wireless network gives your computer Internet access, as well.

Most wireless networks are protected with a security key, which is a kind of password. You need to know the key before attempting to connect. However, after you have connected to the network once, Windows remembers the password and connects again automatically whenever the network comes within range.

Connect to Your Wireless Network

1 Click **Network** (📶).

A Windows displays a list of wireless networks in your area.

2 Click your network.

3 To have Windows connect to your network automatically in the future, click **Connect automatically** (☐ changes to ☑).

4 Click **Connect**.

If the network is protected by a security key, Windows prompts you to enter it.

5 Type the security key.

Ⓑ If you want to be certain that you typed the security key correctly, temporarily click and hold **Display Password Characters** (👁).

6 Click **Next**.

Windows asks if it can locate the other computers and devices on your network.

7 Click **Yes**.

Windows connects to the network.

Ⓒ The network icon changes from Disconnected (📶) to Connected (📶) to indicate that you now have a wireless network connection.

How do I disconnect from my wireless network?

To disconnect from the network, follow these steps:

1 Click **Network** (📶).

2 Click your network.

3 Click **Disconnect**. Windows disconnects from the wireless network.

Switch to a Microsoft Account

You can get much more out of Windows by using a Microsoft account. When you connect a Microsoft account to your Windows user account, many previously inaccessible Windows features become immediately available. For example, you can use the Mail app to access your email and the OneDrive app to store documents online. You can also download apps from the Windows Store, access your photos and documents anywhere online, and even sync your settings with other PCs for which you use the same account.

Switch to a Microsoft Account

Start a Microsoft Account

1 Click **Start** (⊞) (not shown).

2 Click **Settings** (not shown).

Windows opens the Settings app.

3 Click **Accounts**.

The Accounts window appears.

4 Click **Sign in with a Microsoft account instead**.

The Make It Yours window appears.

Configure an Existing Microsoft Account

Ⓐ To create a new Microsoft account, you can click **Create one** and then skip to the next subsection, "Configure a New Microsoft Account."

① Type your email address.

② Type your password.

③ Click **Sign in**.

④ To finish configuring your existing account, skip to the subsection "Complete the Account."

The Let's Create Your Account window appears.

Configure a New Microsoft Account

① Type your name.

② Type the email address you want to use and select either outlook.com or hotmail.com from the list.

③ Type your password.

④ Select your country.

⑤ Type your date of birth.

⑥ Click **Next**.

TIP

Can I use a new Microsoft email address?

Yes, you can. Windows does not require that you use an Outlook.com email address from Microsoft, but you can use such an address if you do not want to use an existing address. In the Let's Create Your Account window, click the **Get a new email address** link and then type the username you want to use with Outlook.com. Your new address will be *username*@outlook.com.

continued ▶

How you proceed after you type your email address depends on whether you are creating a new Microsoft account or using an existing account. Using a Microsoft account with Windows can help if you forget your account password and cannot log in.

You can provide Microsoft with your mobile phone number, so if you ever forget your password, Microsoft will send you a text message to help you reset your password. You can also give Microsoft an alternative email address, or you can provide the answer to a secret question.

Switch to a Microsoft Account (continued)

The Add Security Info window appears.

7 Select your phone number's country code.

8 Type your mobile phone number.

9 Click **Next**.

Complete the Account

Windows asks how you want to receive your security code to verify your account.

1 Click **Next**.

Windows asks you to verify your current account password.

2 Type your password.

3 Click **Next**.

Enter your old password one last time

From here on out, you'll unlock this device using the password or PIN you just set up.

Before we can say goodbye to your local password, you need to provide it one last time.

••••••••••••

(leave blank if none)

Next

Windows asks if you want to use a PIN with your account.

4 Click **Skip this step**.

Note: See Chapter 13 to learn how to add a PIN to your account.

Windows connects the Microsoft account to your user account.

The next time you start Windows, you can use your Microsoft account email address and password to sign in.

Passwords are so yesterday

Using a PIN is faster and more secure than a password—we think you'll love it. How can a short PIN be safer than a long password?

Skip this step

PIN me!

TIP

If I no longer want to use a Microsoft account with Windows, can I remove it?
Yes, you can revert to using your original user account at any time. Note, however, that you will no longer see any personal data on the Start screen, you will not be able to access your files online, and your settings will no longer sync between PCs. To remove the Microsoft account, click **Start** (⊞), click your user name in the upper left corner, and then click **Change account settings**. In the Accounts window, click **Sign in with a local account instead**. Type your Microsoft account password, click **Next**, type your local account password (twice) and a password hint, and click **Next**. Click **Sign out and finish** to complete the removal.

Install an App

If Windows does not come with an app that you need, you can obtain the app and then install it on your computer. How you start the installation process depends on whether you obtained the app from the Windows Store that comes with Windows or you downloaded the app from the Internet. If you purchased the app from a retail store and received a physical copy of the software, you install the app using the CD or DVD disc that comes in the package.

Install an App

Install from the Windows Store

1 Click **Start** (⊞).

2 Click **Store**.

Ⓐ You might also be able to click the Store icon in the taskbar.

Note: You need a Microsoft account to install from the Windows Store, as described in the previous section, "Switch to a Microsoft Account."

The Windows Store appears.

3 Use these tabs or the Search box to locate the app you want to install.

4 Click the app from the results that appear.

5 Click **Free**.

If the app is not free, click the price button instead, type your Microsoft account password, and then click **OK**.

Windows installs the app.

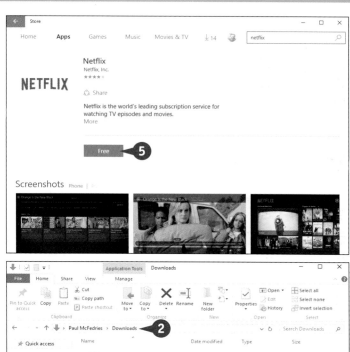

Install a File Downloaded from the Internet

1 Click **File Explorer** (📁).

2 Click **Downloads**.

Note: If you saved the downloaded file in a folder other than Downloads, use File Explorer to find the downloaded file. To view a file with File Explorer, see Chapter 10.

The Downloads folder appears.

3 Double-click the file.

The software's installation app begins.

Note: For compressed files, extract the files and then double-click the setup file. See Chapter 10 for more information.

4 Follow the installation instructions the app provides.

How do I install software from a CD or DVD?
Insert the disc and, when the AutoPlay dialog box appears, click **Run *file***, where *file* is the name of the installation app (usually SETUP. EXE). Then follow the installation instructions the app provides (these installation steps vary from app to app).

How do I find my software's product key or serial number?
Look for a sticker attached to the back or inside of the CD case. Also look on the registration card, on the CD, or on the back of the box. If you downloaded the app, the number should appear on the download screen and on the email receipt you receive.

Start an App

To perform tasks of any kind in Windows, you can use one of the apps installed on your computer. The application you use depends on the task you want to perform. For example, if you want to surf the World Wide Web, you use a web browser application, such as the Microsoft Edge app that comes with Windows.

Before you can use an application, however, you must first tell Windows which application you want to run. You can start an app either from the Start menu or from the All Apps list.

Start an App

Using the Start Menu

1 Click **Start** (⊞).

A Your most frequently used apps appear here.

B Common Windows features appear here.

C The right side of the Start menu displays *tiles* for commonly used apps.

2 Click the app you want to start.

The app runs.

D To close an app, you can click **Close** (✕) or press **Alt** + **F4**.

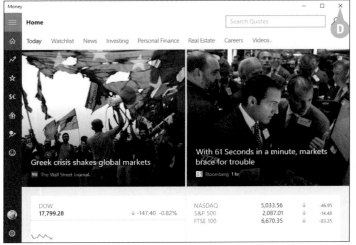

Using the All Apps List

1 Click **Start** (⊞).

2 Click **All apps**.

E After you click All Apps, the name changes to Back.

3 Click the icon for the program you want to launch.

F If your program icon is in a submenu, click the submenu and then click the program icon.

Windows launches the app.

Is there an easier way to locate an app?

Yes, you can perform a search to locate it. Click inside the taskbar's Search box and then begin typing the name of the app. As you type, Windows displays a list of apps and other items that match the characters. When you see the app you want, click it to run the program.

What are tiles?

A tile is a method for displaying a shortcut that launches an app. Many tiles are *live*, which means that a tile's text changes to display the app's most recent information, such as the latest news or your most recently received email messages. See the section "Pin an App to the Start Menu" in Chapter 2 to learn how to add your own Start menu tiles.

Switch Between Running Apps

If you plan on running multiple applications at the same time, you need to know how to easily switch from one application to another. In Windows, after you start one application, you do not need to close that application before you open another one. Windows supports a feature called *multitasking*, which means running two or more applications at once. For example, you might keep your word processing application, your web browser, and your email application open all day. You can switch from one program to another using either the taskbar or the keyboard.

Switch Between Running Apps

Switch Apps Using the Taskbar

① Move the mouse (👆) over the taskbar button of the program you want to switch to.

🅐 Windows displays a thumbnail version of the app window.

② Click the app's taskbar button.

Note: A program does not have to be minimized to the taskbar for you to use the program's taskbar button.

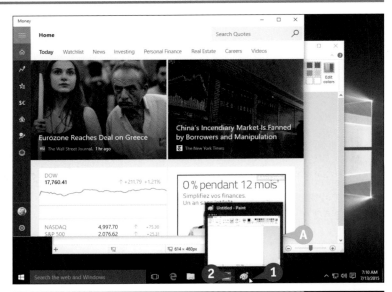

🅑 Windows brings the program's window to the foreground.

Note: You can also switch to another window by clicking the window, even if it is in the background.

Switch Apps Using Task View

1 In the taskbar, click **Task View** (▢).

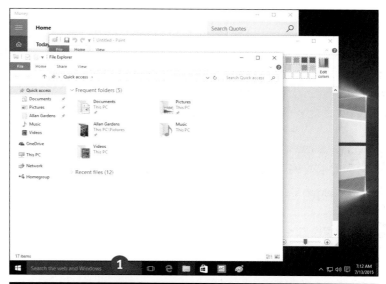

C Windows displays thumbnails for each running program.

2 Click the thumbnail of the program you want to switch to.

Windows switches to the program.

TIPS

Is there an easy way to arrange windows so they do not overlap?

Yes, you can *snap* windows into place. To snap a window to the left half of the screen, drag the top of the window until the mouse (↖) hits the left edge of the screen, and then release. Similarly, drag a window to the right edge to snap it to the right. To snap a window to a quarter of the screen, drag the window to any corner.

How can I switch between apps using the keyboard?

Press and hold **Alt** and then press **Tab** to see thumbnail versions of the open windows. Press **Tab** until the window you want to work in is selected and then release **Alt**.

Update an App

You can ensure that you are using the latest version of an app by using the Windows Store to install an available update. After a software company releases an app, its programmers continue to work on it. They add new features, improve existing features, fix problems, and close security holes.

After fully testing these improvements and fixes, they place the new version of the app in the Windows Store, which alerts you that an update is available. You can then install the new version.

Update an App

1 Click **Start** (⊞).

2 Click **Store**.

The Windows Store app appears.

A This number tells you how many updates are available.

3 Click **Updates** (↓).

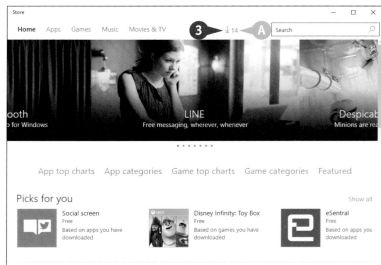

The Windows Store displays a list of the available updates.

④ To ensure that you are seeing all the available updates, click **Check for updates**.

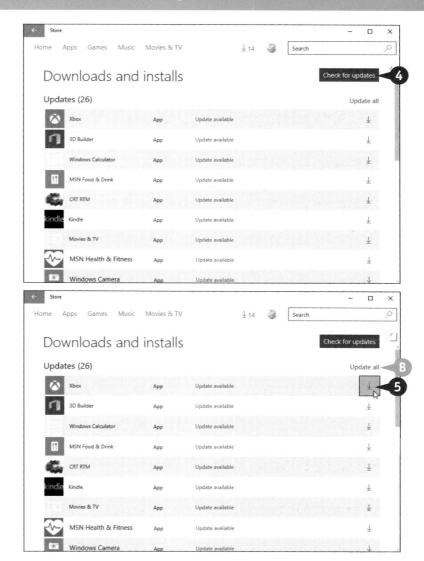

Ⓑ If you prefer to update all the apps at once, click **Update all** and skip step **5**.

⑤ Click **Update** (↓).

Windows installs the app updates.

TIPS

Can I automate the updates?
Yes. Instead of updating your apps manually, configure Windows to update the apps automatically. In the Store app, click your user icon, click **Settings**, and then click the **Update apps automatically** switch to **On**.

How do I update Windows?
By default, Windows is configured to automatically check for updated system files each day. If updates are available, Windows downloads and installs them. If you know of an important update, you can check for it manually if you would rather not wait for the automatic check. Click **Start** (⊞) and then click **Settings** to open the Settings app. Click **Update & security** and then click **Check for updates**.

Uninstall an App

If you have an app that you no longer use, you can free up some hard drive space and reduce clutter on the Start screen by uninstalling that app. When you install an app, the program stores its files on your computer's hard drive, and although most programs are quite small, many require hundreds of megabytes of hard drive space. Uninstalling an app you do not need frees up the hard drive space it uses and removes its tile (or tiles) from the Start screen (if it has any there) and the Apps screen.

Uninstall an App

Uninstall via the Start Menu

1 Click **Start** (⊞).

2 Use the Start menu or the All Apps list to locate the app you want to uninstall.

3 Right-click the app.

4 Click **Uninstall**.

Windows asks you to confirm.

5 Click **Uninstall**.

Windows removes the app.

Uninstall via Programs and Features

1 Type **uninstall**.

2 Click **Change or remove a program**.

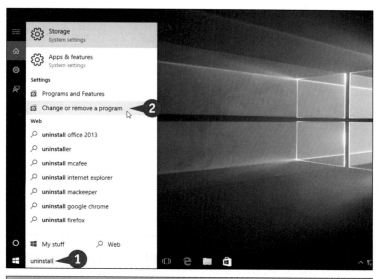

The Programs and Features window appears.

3 Click the app you want to uninstall.

4 Click **Uninstall** (or **Uninstall/Change**).

The app's uninstall procedure begins.

5 Follow the instructions on the screen, which vary from app to app.

How can I uninstall the app that is taking up the most space?

Click **Start** (⊞) and then click **Settings** to open the Settings app. Click **System** and then click **Apps & features** to see a list of apps sorted by size. To remove an app, click it, click **Uninstall**, and then click **Uninstall** when Windows asks you to confirm.

What is the difference between an Automatic and a Custom uninstall?

The Automatic uninstall requires no input from you. It is the easiest, safest choice and therefore the one you should choose. The Custom uninstall gives you more control, but it is more complex and suitable only for experienced users.

CHAPTER 2

Customizing Windows

Windows comes with a number of features that enable you to personalize your computer. Not only can you change the appearance of Windows to suit your taste, but you can also change the way Windows works to make it easier to use and more efficient.

Pin an App to the Start Menu

You can customize the Start menu to gain quick access to the programs that you use most often. If you have an app that does not appear on the Start menu, you usually open the app by clicking the Start menu's All Apps command and then negotiating the menus and submenus that appear. For the apps you use most often, you can avoid this extra work by *pinning* their icons permanently to the right side of the main Start menu. After you have pinned an app, you can launch it by displaying the Start menu and clicking the app.

Pin an App to the Start Menu

1 Click **Start** (⊞).

2 Locate the app that you want to pin to the Start menu.

3 Right-click the app.

The app shortcut menu appears.

4 Click **Pin to Start**.

A A tile for the pinned app appears on the right side of the Start menu.

Note: To remove an app tile from the Start menu, click **Start** (⊞), right-click the tile, and then click **Unpin from Start**.

TIPS

Can I move an app tile within the Start menu?
Yes, you can move any app tile to a different position within the Start menu. To move a tile, click **Start** (⊞), press and hold the mouse button as you drag the tile to its new position, and then release the mouse button.

Can I change the size of a Start menu tile?
Yes. In all cases, you can select either a Small or Medium square. With some apps, you can also choose either a Wide rectangle or a Large square. To change the size, click **Start** (⊞), right-click the app's tile, click **Resize**, and then click the size you want.

Open the Settings App

You can configure and customize many aspects of your Windows system using the Settings app. Settings is the Windows app that you use for customizing and tweaking your PC. Many of the tasks that follow in this chapter, including changing the Lock screen backgrounds and adding an app to the Lock screen, are performed using the Settings app. Settings also offers a wealth of other options that you can use to customize your PC.

You open Settings either via the Start menu or via the Charms menu of some Windows apps.

Open the Settings App

Open the Settings App

1 Click **Start** (⊞).

2 Click **Settings**.

The Settings app appears.

Note: You can also open the Settings app by pressing ⊞+🔲.

Navigate the Settings App

1 Click a category.

The Settings app displays the category.

2 Click a tab.

3 Use the controls on the right side of the app window to modify the tab's settings.

Windows puts the new settings into effect.

A You can click **Back** (←) if you need to return to the previous Settings screen.

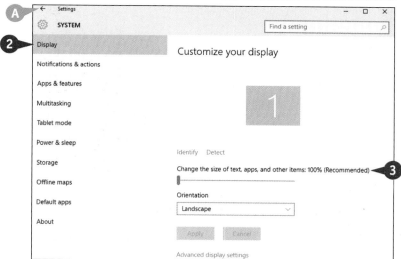

TIP

If I know which tab of the Settings app I want to use, is there a quick way to display it?

Yes, you can use the taskbar's Search box, which enables you to quickly search for the setting that you want to work with. Click inside the Search box and then begin typing the name of the tab or setting you want.

For example, if you want to go directly to the Accounts tab, type **accounts** and then click **Add, delete, and manage other user accounts** in the search results. Note that Settings items appear in the search results with the Settings icon (⚙).

Change the Lock Screen Background

You can make your Lock screen more interesting by changing the image that appears as its background. Locking your computer is a useful safety feature because it prevents unauthorized users from accessing your files and your network. If you find yourself looking at the Lock screen frequently, you might prefer to see something other than the default image. Windows comes with several system pictures that you can use, or you can use one of your own pictures.

Change the Lock Screen Background

1 Open the Settings app.

Note: See the previous section, "Open the Settings App."

2 Click **Personalization**.

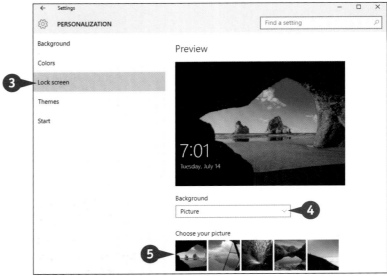

The Personalization settings appear.

3 Click **Lock screen.**

4 Click the **Background ˅** and then click **Picture**.

5 To use a default image, click the thumbnail of the picture that you want to use.

6 To use one of your own pictures, click **Browse**.

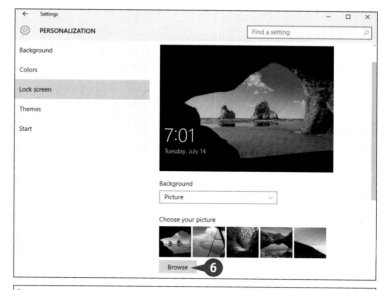

7 Click the picture that you want to use.

8 Click **Choose picture**.

The image appears the next time that you lock your computer.

TIP

How do I lock my computer?
Click **Start** (⊞), click your username at the top of the menu, and then click **Lock**. You can also press ⊞+🅛. You can configure Windows to automatically lock the computer after it has been idle for a specified amount of time. In the Search box, type **lock the computer**. Click **Lock the computer when I leave it alone for a period of time**. Click **On resume, display logon screen** (☐ changes to ☑). Use the Wait text box to set the number of minutes of idle time after which Windows locks your PC. Click **OK**.

Add an App to the Lock Screen

When you lock your PC, Windows displays status icons for some apps. For example, the status icon for the Mail app shows the number of unread messages. The Lock screen also shows any new notifications that appear for the Calendar app, such as an upcoming appointment. If you lock your computer frequently, you can make the Lock screen even more useful by adding icons for other apps, including ones that support notifications.

Add an App to the Lock Screen

1 Open the Settings app.

Note: See the section "Open the Settings App" earlier in this chapter.

2 Click **Personalization**.

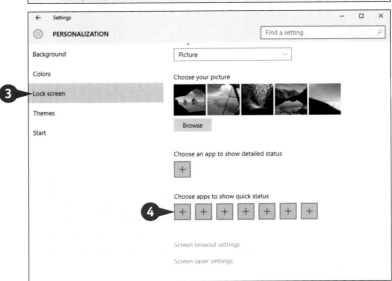

The Personalization settings appear.

3 Click **Lock screen**.

4 To set a quick status icon for an app, click a button.

The Choose an App window appears.

5 Click the app for which you want to add a quick status icon to the Lock screen.

6 Repeat steps **4** and **5** to set the other quick status icons.

Ⓐ If you do not want an app associated with the icon, click **None**.

7 To choose which app displays its detailed status, click here.

8 Click the app.

Ⓑ If you do not want a detailed status, click **None**.

Windows puts the new settings into effect, and the apps appear on the Lock screen the next time that you use it.

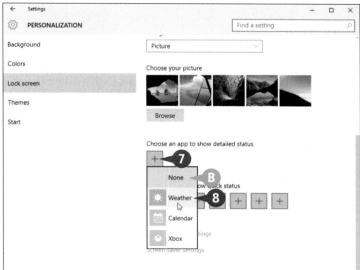

TIP

What is the difference between a quick status and detailed status?
A *quick status* means that the Lock screen shows only a small icon for an app, and that icon displays the number of recent or unread items, such as the number of unread email messages in the Mail app. A *detailed status* means that the Lock screen shows more information from the app. For example, if you have an upcoming event in the Calendar app, the Lock screen shows the details of that event, including the event title, location, and time.

Synchronize Settings Between PCs

If, besides your Windows desktop computer, you also have a Windows notebook, a Windows tablet, and a Windows smartphone, using the same Microsoft account on each platform means that you can synchronize data among them. You can sync customizations, such as backgrounds and themes; system settings, such as languages and regional settings; Microsoft Edge data, such as favorites and history; and app settings and more. This gives you a consistent interface across your devices and consistent data so that you can be more productive.

Synchronize Settings Between PCs

1 Open the Settings app.

Note: See the section "Open the Settings App" earlier in this chapter.

2 Click **Accounts**.

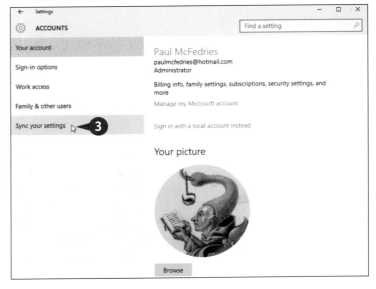

The Accounts settings appear.

3 Click **Sync your settings**.

The Sync settings appear.

④ Click the **Sync settings** switch to **On**.

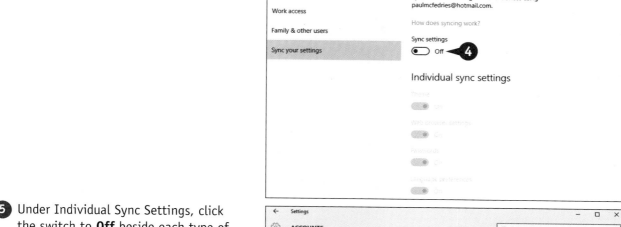

⑤ Under Individual Sync Settings, click the switch to **Off** beside each type of setting that you do not want to include in the sync.

The next time Windows syncs, it does not include the settings that you turned off.

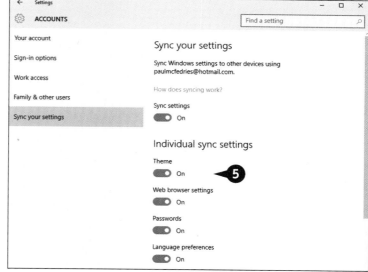

Why is the Passwords switch disabled on my Sync Your Settings screen?

This occurs when you have yet to verify your identity on your PC. Verifying your identity means having a confirmation code sent to the mobile phone number associated with your Microsoft account. To verify your identity, use the taskbar's Search box to type **actions** and then click **View recommended actions to keep Windows running smoothly**. In the Security and Maintenance window that appears, you should see the message "Verify your identity on this PC." Click **Verify** to the right of that message, and then follow the instructions that appear for having the confirmation code sent to your mobile phone.

Access an App's Features

Depending on the app, you might see a few tabs across the top of the window, as well as a Search box in the upper-right corner of the window. However, almost all the apps that come with Windows include a strip running down the left side of the window. This is the app menu, and it gives you access to a number of features, including commands, settings, and views. This menu shows only icons at first, but you can open the menu to display the names of each feature. You can then click the feature that you want to use.

Access an App's Features

Display the Menu

1 Open the app that you want to work with.

2 Click **Menu** (☰).

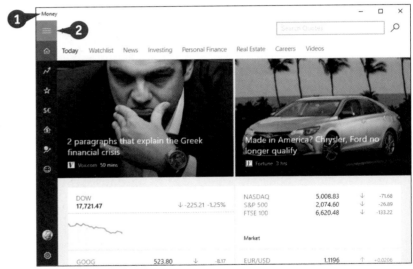

A The app menu expands to show the feature names.

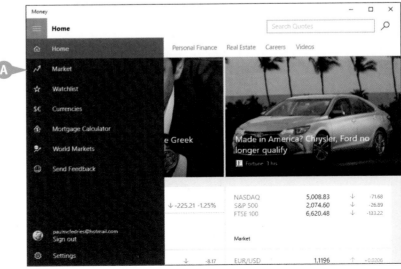

Hide the Menu

Note: If you click a menu feature, the app automatically hides the menu. You need to manually hide the menu if you decide not to select a feature.

1 Click **Menu** (≡).

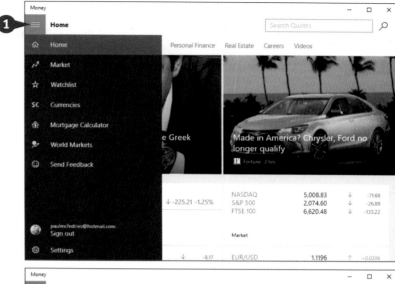

B The app hides the menu.

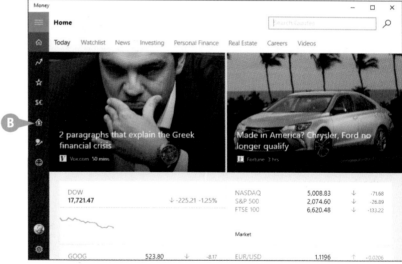

Do all apps use the Menu icon?

No. The so-called *Modern* apps that ship with Windows — including Mail, Calendar, People, Maps, News, and Weather — use the Menu icon (≡), as do some third-party apps. However, the so-called *Desktop* apps — including File Explorer, Paint, and WordPad — do not use this feature.

Are there more app features that I can access?

Yes, you can also display the Settings pane for each app. The layout of the Settings pane varies between apps, but it usually includes commands for setting app preferences and options. To display an app's Settings pane, click **Menu** (≡) and then click **Settings** (⚙).

Pin an App to the Taskbar

Pinning an app to the Start menu, as described earlier in this chapter, is helpful because it puts the app just two clicks away. If you have an app that you use frequently, you might prefer to have that app just a single click away. You can achieve this by pinning the app to the taskbar. You can pin an app to the taskbar either from the Start menu or from the taskbar itself.

Pin an App to the Taskbar

Using the Start Menu

1 Click **Start** (⊞).

2 If you do not see the app you want to pin, click **All apps**.

3 Locate the app that you want to pin to the taskbar.

4 Right-click the app.

5 Click **Pin to taskbar**.

Ⓐ An icon for the app now appears in the taskbar.

Using the Taskbar

❶ Launch the app that you want to pin to the taskbar.

❷ Right-click the running app's taskbar icon.

❸ Click **Pin this program to taskbar**.

❹ Click **Close** (✖).

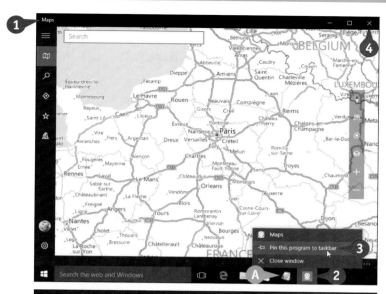

Ⓑ An icon for the app remains on the taskbar.

Can I change the order of the taskbar icons?
Yes. Click and drag a taskbar icon to the left or right and then drop it in the new position. Note that this technique applies not only to the icons pinned to the taskbar, but also to the icons for any running programs.

How do I remove an app icon from the taskbar?
If you decide that you no longer require an app to be pinned to the taskbar, you should remove it to reduce taskbar clutter and provide more room for other app icons. To remove a pinned app icon, right-click the icon and then click **Unpin this program from taskbar**.

Adjust the Volume

While an audio or video file is playing, you can adjust the volume up or down to get its audio just right. If you are listening to media by yourself, you can adjust the volume to suit the music and your mood. However, if there are other people nearby, you will probably want to use the volume control to keep the playback volume low to avoid disturbing them. If you need to silence the media temporarily, you can mute the playback.

Adjust the Volume

1. In the taskbar, click **Volume** (🔊).

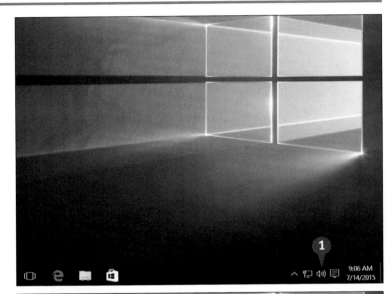

The Volume window appears.

2. Click and drag the slider to set the volume level that you want.

A. You can also click **Mute** (🔊) to mute the volume (🔊 changes to 🔇).

Windows sets the system volume to the new level.

Set the Time Zone

To ensure that your system clock is accurate, you should set the time zone to correspond to your location. When Windows configures your computer, it performs a number of chores, including setting the current system time and time zone. However, for the time zone, Windows defaults to Pacific Time in North America. If this is not the time zone used where you live, you must select the correct one to ensure that you have the accurate system time.

Set the Time Zone

1 Open the Settings app.

Note: See the section "Open the Settings App" earlier in this chapter.

2 Click **Time & language**.

3 Click the **Time zone** ⌄ and then click your time zone.

Windows adjusts the time to the new time zone.

Configure Windows to Work with Multiple Monitors

You can improve your productivity and efficiency by using a second monitor. To work with an extra monitor, your PC must have a second video output port, such as VGA, DVI, or HDMI. If you do not have such a port, check with the manufacturer to see if an adapter is available that enables your PC to connect with an extra monitor.

After you have connected your PC and the external monitor, you then need to configure Windows to extend the Start screen to both the main screen and the second monitor.

Configure Windows to Work with Multiple Monitors

1 Connect the second monitor to your PC.

2 Open the Settings app.

Note: See the section "Open the Settings App" earlier in this chapter.

3 Click **System**.

The System settings appear.

4 Click **Display**.

5 Click the **Multiple displays** ∨.

6 Click **Extend these displays**.

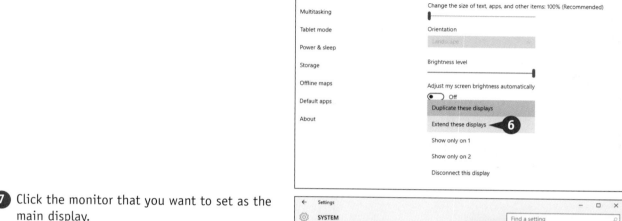

7 Click the monitor that you want to set as the main display.

8 Click **Make this my main display** (☐ changes to ☑).

9 Click **Apply**.

Windows connects to the second monitor and uses the selected monitor as your main display.

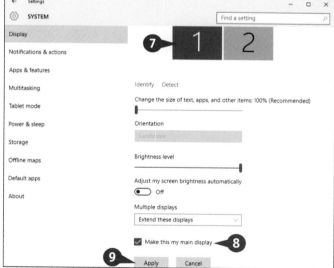

TIPS

Why does my mouse pointer stop at the right edge of the left screen?

This means that you need to exchange the icons of the left and right monitors. To do that, click and drag the left monitor icon to the right of the other monitor icon (or vice versa).

How do I configure Windows to stop using the external monitor?

Follow steps **2** to **4** in this section to open the Multiple Displays list and then click **Show only on 1**. You can also usually revert to using just the original PC screen by disconnecting the monitor from your computer.

Customize the Taskbar's Notification Area

Y ou can customize how Windows displays the taskbar's notification area icons to ensure a particular icon is always visible or to turn off an icon's notifications.

The notification area shows only a few icons by default: Network, Volume, and Notifications, and notebook PCs also show the Power icon. You might want to customize the default arrangement. For example, many notification icons offer quick access to their programs' features when you right-click them. If there is an icon that you right-click frequently, you might want to configure the notification area to show the icon on the taskbar.

Customize the Taskbar's Notification Area

1 In the taskbar's Search box, type **notifications**.

2 Click **Notifications & actions settings**.

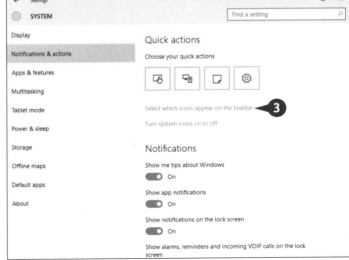

The Settings app displays the Notifications & Actions window.

3 Click **Select which icons appear on the taskbar**.

The Select Which Icons Appear on the Taskbar window appears.

④ Click the switch to **On** for each icon you want to display in the notification area.

⑤ Click **Back** (←) to return to the Notifications & Actions window.

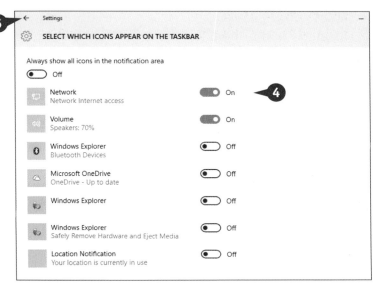

⑥ Click **Turn system icons on or off** (not shown).

⑦ Click the switch to **Off** for each system icon you want to prevent from appearing in the notification area.

Windows puts the new settings into effect.

Ⓐ You can click **Show hidden icons** (⌃) to see your hidden icons.

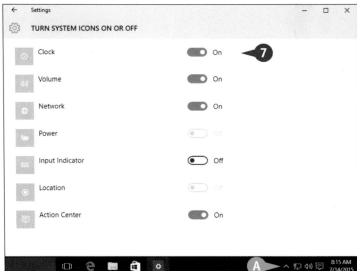

Is there a faster way to show every icon on the taskbar?
Yes. Follow steps **1** to **3** to open the Select Which Icons Appear on the Taskbar window. Click the **Always show all icons in the notification area** switch to **On**.

Can I configure the taskbar to always appear on the screen?
Yes. The default taskbar state is hidden, and you display it by moving the mouse (▷) to the bottom of the screen. This gives you more desktop room, but if you would prefer not to perform this extra step to display the taskbar, right-click the taskbar, click **Properties**, and then click **Auto-hide the taskbar** (☑ changes to ☐). Click **OK**.

Set Up Multiple Desktops

You can make your PC screen easier to manage and less cluttered by organizing your running programs into two or more desktops. Each desktop includes only the windows of the programs that you have assigned to that desktop. For example, you might have a work desktop that includes only a word processor, a spreadsheet, and Microsoft Edge for research; a social desktop that includes only Mail, People, and Calendar; and a media desktop that includes only Music, Photos, and Videos. You can quickly switch from one desktop to another.

Set Up Multiple Desktops

Add a New Desktop

1 In the taskbar, click **Task view** (▣).

2 Click **New desktop**.

Ⓐ Windows creates a new desktop.

Ⓑ Your original desktop is shown as Desktop 1.

Switch to Another Desktop

1 In the taskbar, click **Task view** (▣) (not shown).

C Position the mouse (↖) over the other desktop to see the programs running within that desktop.

2 Click the desktop you want to use.

Windows switches to that desktop and displays its running programs.

Note: Any new programs you launch will now appear only in the selected desktop.

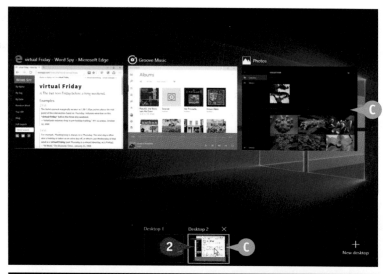

Move a Program to a Different Desktop

1 In the taskbar, click **Task view** (▣) (not shown).

2 Right-click the program you want to move.

3 Click **Move to**.

4 Click the desktop to which you want the program moved.

D You can also click **New Desktop** to move the program to a new desktop.

Windows moves the program to the selected desktop.

What shortcut methods I can use?

Press ⊞+Tab to open Task view. To switch between desktops, open Task view, press Tab to select a desktop thumbnail, use ← and → to highlight the desktop you want, and then press Enter. You can also press ⊞+Ctrl+D to create a new desktop and ⊞+Ctrl+F4 to close the current desktop.

How do I close a desktop?

Click **Task view** (▣) to display the desktop thumbnails. Move the mouse (↖) over the desktop you want to close and then click **Close** (✖) in the upper left corner of the desktop thumbnail. Windows closes the desktop. If the desktop contained running programs, they are assigned to your original desktop.

CHAPTER 3

Surfing the Web

This chapter shows you how to use Microsoft Edge (which replaces Internet Explorer in Windows 10) to navigate from site to site. You learn how to enter web page addresses, work with tabs, save your favorite sites, search for information, and more.

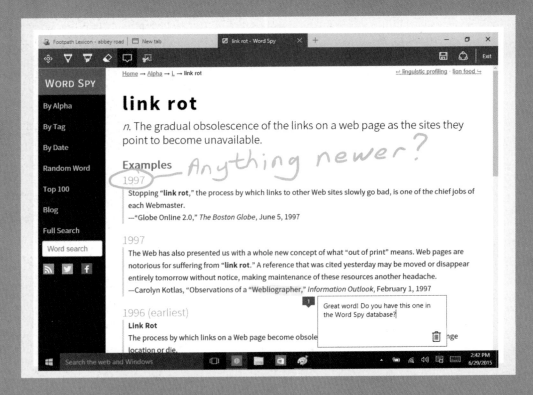

Open a Web Page

Although you usually navigate web pages by clicking links, if you know the address of a specific page, you can type it into the web browser to display it. Every web page is uniquely identified by an address composed of four basic parts: the transfer method (usually http, which stands for *Hypertext Transfer Protocol*), the website domain name, the directory where the web page is located on the server, and the web page filename. The website domain name suffix most often used is .com (commercial), but other common suffixes include .gov (government), .org (nonprofit organization), .edu (education), and country domains such as .ca (Canada).

Open a Web Page

Enter a Web Page Address

1 Click **Microsoft Edge** (🄴).

2 Click in the address bar.

3 Type the address of the web page.

4 Click **Go** (→).

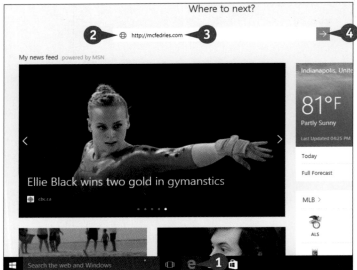

The web page appears.

Ⓐ If you find that Microsoft Edge cannot display the page, this is usually a temporary glitch, so click **Refresh** (↻) to try loading the page again.

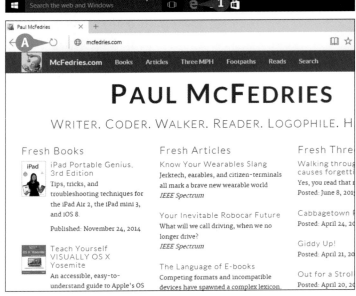

Select a Link

1 Position the mouse (⬚) over a link (⬚ changes to 🖑).

2 Click the link.

B The Status area shows the link address.

Note: The address shown in the status bar when you point at a link may be different than the one shown when the page is downloading. This happens when the website "redirects" the link, which happens often.

The linked web page appears.

C The web page title and address change after the linked page is loaded.

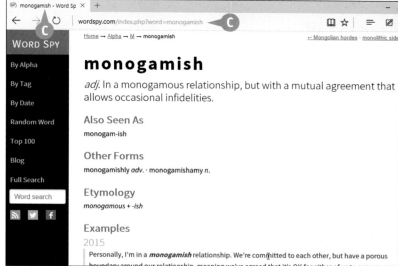

TIP

Are there any shortcuts that I can use to enter web page addresses?
Yes. Here are some useful keyboard techniques:

- After you finish typing the address, press `Enter` instead of clicking **Go** (→).
- Most web addresses begin with *http://*. You can leave off these characters when you type your address.
- If the address uses the form http://www.*something*.com, type just the *something* part and then press `Ctrl` + `Enter`. Microsoft Edge automatically adds *http://www.* at the beginning and *.com* at the end.

Open a Web Page in a Tab

Ah s you surf the web, you may come upon a page that you want to keep available while you visit other sites. That page may contain important information that you need to reference, or it might be a page that you want to read later on.

Instead of leaving the page and trying to find it again later, Microsoft Edge lets you keep the page open in a special section of the browser screen called a *tab*. You can use a second tab to visit your other sites and then resume viewing the first site by clicking its tab.

Open a Web Page in a Tab

Open a Web Page in a Tab

1 Right-click the link you want to open.

2 Click **Open in new tab**.

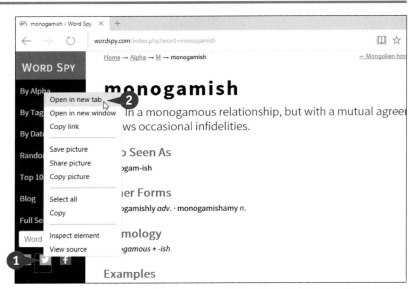

A A new tab appears with the page title.

3 Click the tab to display the page.

B You can also create a new tab by clicking **New Tab** (+).

Navigate Tabs

1 Click **Scroll tab list backward** (<)
or **Scroll tab list forward** (>) to
display the tab you want.

Note: You see the tab scroll buttons
only if Microsoft Edge does not have
enough room to display all the tabs.

2 Click the tab.

C The web page loaded in the tab
appears.

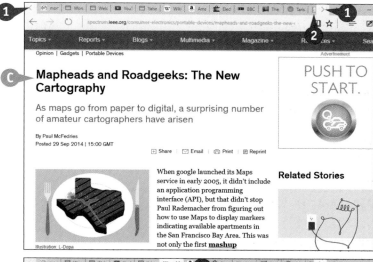

Close a Tab

1 Position the mouse () over the
tab you want to close.

2 Click **Close Tab** ().

Are there any shortcuts I can use to open web pages in tabs?

Here are some useful keyboard techniques:

- Press and hold `Ctrl` and click a link to open the page in a tab.
- Press and hold `Ctrl`+`Shift` and click a link to open the page in a tab and display the tab.
- Type an address and then press `Alt`+`Enter` to open the page in a new tab.
- Press `Ctrl`+`Tab` or `Ctrl`+`Shift`+`Tab` to cycle through the tabs.
- Press `Ctrl`+`W` to close the current tab.
- Press `Ctrl`+`Alt`+`F4` to close every tab but the current one.

Navigate Web Pages

After you have visited several pages, you can return to a page that you visited earlier. Instead of retyping the address or looking for the link, Microsoft Edge gives you some easier methods.

When you navigate from page to page, you create a kind of "path" through the web. Microsoft Edge keeps track of this path by maintaining a list of the pages that you have visited. You can use that list to go back to a page. After you have gone back, you can also use that same list to go forward through the pages again.

Navigate Web Pages

Go Back

1 To go back one page, click **Back** (←).

The page appears.

Go Forward

1 To go forward one page, click **Forward** (→).

Note: If you are at the last page viewed up to that point, Forward (→) is not active.

The page appears.

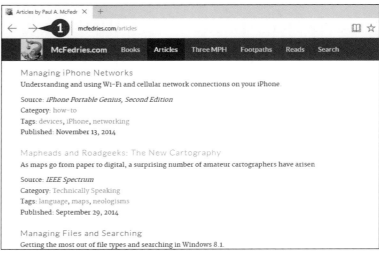

Find Text on a Page

When you are reading a page on the web, it is not unusual to be looking for specific information. In those situations, rather than read through the entire page to find the information you are looking for, you can search the web page text for the data. The Find on Page feature in Microsoft Edge lets you to do that by enabling you to search through the current page text for a specific word or phrase.

Find Text on a Page

1 Click **More** (⋯).

2 Click **Find on page**.

You can also press **Ctrl** + **F**.

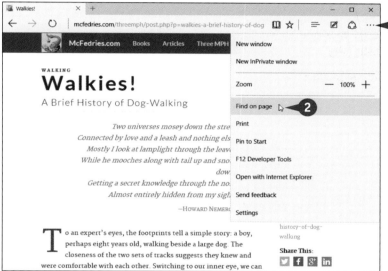

The Find on Page bar appears.

3 Type the word or phrase that you want to locate.

A Microsoft Edge highlights the matching text on the page.

B You can click **Next** (>) to cycle forward through the matches.

C You can click **Previous** (<) to cycle backward through the matches.

4 When you are done, click **Close** (✕).

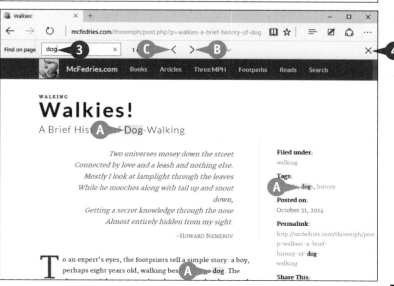

Navigate with the History List

Back and Forward (← and →) enable you to navigate pages only in the current browser session. To redisplay sites that you have visited in the past few days or weeks, you need to use the History list, which is a collection of the websites and pages you have visited over the past month.

If you visit sensitive places such as an Internet banking site or your corporate site, you can increase security by clearing the History list so that other people cannot see where you have been.

Navigate with the History List

1 Click **Hub** (≡).

2 Click **History** (🕚).

A The History list appears.

3 Click the day or week that you visited the site.

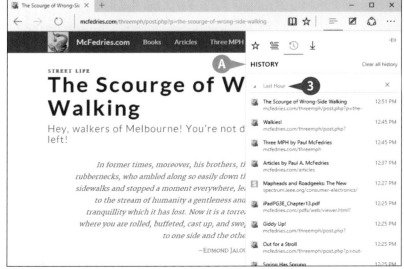

A list of pages you visited during that day or week appears.

④ Click the page you want to display.

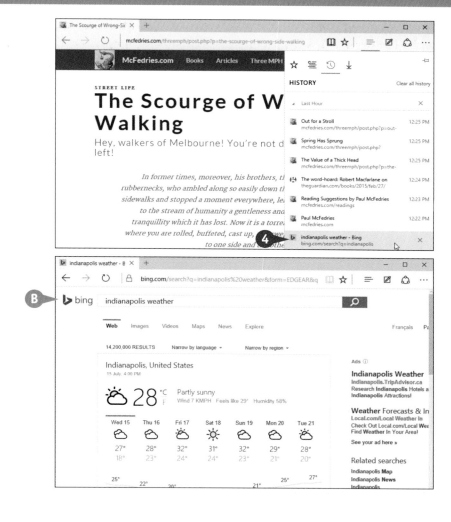

Ⓑ The page appears.

Change Your Startup Page

Your startup page is the screen, web page, or collection of tabs that appears when you first start Microsoft Edge. The default startup page is the New Tab page, which displays a list of common sites and some suggested content. However, you can configure Microsoft Edge to open a specific web page or a collection of tabs as the startup page.

Change Your Startup Page

1 Click **More** (⋯).

2 Click **Settings**.

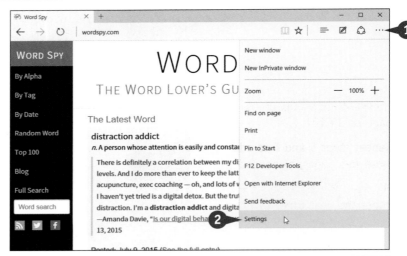

The Settings pane appears.

3 Click **A specific page or pages** (○ changes to ◉).

4 Click ∨ and then click **Custom**.

5 Type the web page address.

6 Click **Add** (+).

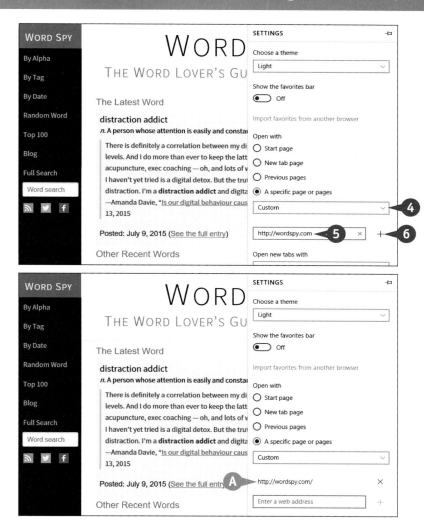

Ⓐ Microsoft Edge adds the web page to the list.

7 Repeat steps **5** and **6** to add more web pages, as needed.

Microsoft Edge displays these pages the next time you start the app.

TIPS

Can I get Microsoft Edge to load a tab without displaying a startup page?
Yes. Follow steps **1** and **2** to open the Settings pane. Click the **Open new tabs with** ∨ and then click **A blank page**.

How can I get Microsoft Edge to open with the pages I was using when I last closed it?
Follow steps **1** and **2** to open the Settings pane. In the Open With section, click **Previous pages** (○ changes to ●). The next time you start Microsoft Edge, it will redisplay the pages you had open in tabs the last time.

Save Favorite Web Pages

If you have web pages that you visit frequently, you can save yourself time by saving those pages as favorites within Microsoft Edge. This enables you to display the pages with just a couple of clicks.

You save favorite pages in Microsoft Edge by adding them to a special section of the app called the Favorites list. Instead of typing an address or searching for one of these pages, you can display the web page by clicking it in the Favorites list.

Save Favorite Web Pages

Save a Favorite Web Page

1 Display the web page you want to save as a favorite.

2 Click **Add to favorites** (☆).

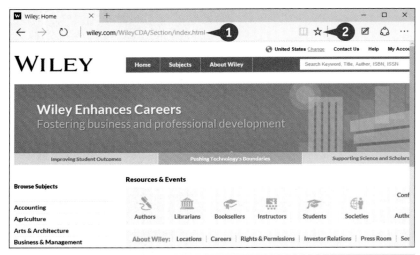

The Add to Favorites dialog box appears.

Note: You can also display the Add to Favorites dialog box by pressing `Ctrl`+`D`.

3 Edit the page name, as necessary.

4 Click **Add**.

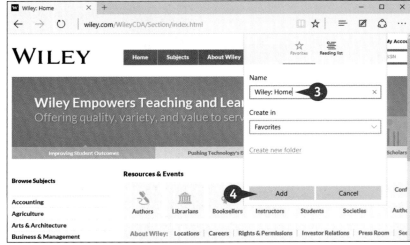

Display a Favorite Web Page

1 Click **Hub** (☰).

2 Click **Favorites** (☆).

The Favorites list appears.

3 Click the web page you want to display.

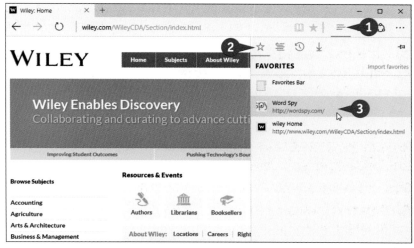

A The web page appears.

B If you use your Favorites list a lot, you can make it easier to display the pages by keeping the Hub visible. Click **Hub** (☰) and then click **Pin the Hub** (⊣). Microsoft Edge pins the Hub to the right side of the window.

TIPS

Is there an easy way to organize my favorites?
Yes, you can create Hub folders for storing related favorites. For example, you could create a folder for work, another for each of your hobbies, and so on. Follow steps **1** to **3** and then click **Create a folder**. Type a name for the folder and then click **Add** to save the favorite in that folder.

How do I delete a favorite?
If the site is on the Favorites bar, right-click the favorite and then click **Remove**. For all other favorites, click **Hub** (☰), click **Favorites** (☆), right-click the favorite you want to delete, and then click **Remove**.

Take Advantage of the Favorites Bar

Y̲ou can use Microsoft Edge's Favorites bar to provide easy one-click access to those websites that you visit most often.

One of Microsoft Edge's most useful features is the Favorites bar, which appears below the address box. The Favorites bar is fully customizable, which means you can populate the Favorites bar with new buttons associated with the sites you visit most often. This section shows you how to display and populate the Favorites bar and takes you through a few Favorites bar customizations.

Take Advantage of the Favorites Bar

Display the Favorites Bar

1 Click **More** (⋯).

2 Click **Settings**.

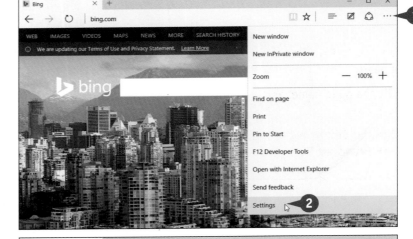

The Settings pane appears.

3 Click the **Show the favorites bar** switch to **On**.

Ⓐ Microsoft Edge displays the Favorites bar.

4 Click outside the Settings pane to close it

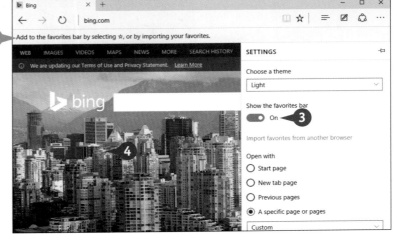

Add a Web Page to the Favorites Bar

1 Navigate to the page that contains the link you want to add to the Favorites bar.

2 Click **Add to favorites** (☆).

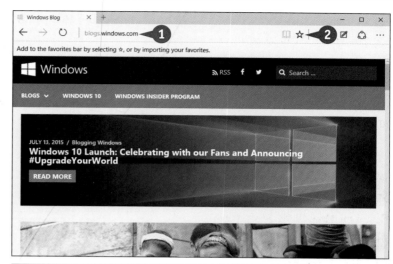

The Add to Favorites dialog box appears.

3 Edit the page name, as necessary.

4 Click the **Create in** ⌄ and then click **Favorites Bar**.

5 Click **Add**.

B Microsoft Edge adds the web page to the Favorites bar.

TIPS

Can I move or delete Favorites bar buttons?

Yes. To move a button, click and drag the button left or right and then drop it in the new position. To delete a button, right-click it and then click **Remove**.

How do I change the name of a button?

By default, Microsoft Edge uses the page title as the name of the Favorites bar button. If you do not like the default name, or if you would prefer something shorter or more descriptive, click **Hub** (≡), click **Favorites** (☆), and then click **Favorites Bar**. Right-click the button you want to edit, click **Rename**, type the new name, and then press Enter.

Create Web Notes

The Web Notes feature enables you to mark up a web page by annotating and highlighting page elements, adding your own text notes, and clipping part of the page.

When you read a paper document, you might often mark up the page with proofreading symbols, highlight passages, and add your own notes in the margins. Microsoft Edge offers Web Notes, which give you the same capabilities when you are reading a web page. These annotations are stored in Microsoft Edge, where you can view them or copy them to other apps.

Create Web Notes

Display the Web Note Tools

1. Navigate to the page you want to annotate.

2. Click **Make a Web Note** (📝).

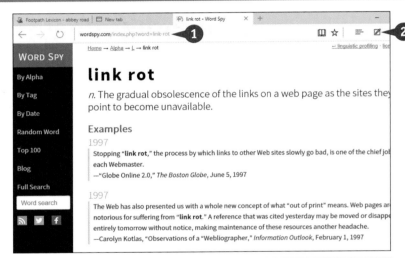

A. Microsoft Edge displays the Web Note tools.

Annotate a Web Page

1. Click the annotation tool you want to use:

B. Click **Pen** (📝) to draw lines or handwrite text.

C. Click **Highlighter** (📝) to highlight page elements.

2. Click and drag on the page to create the annotation.

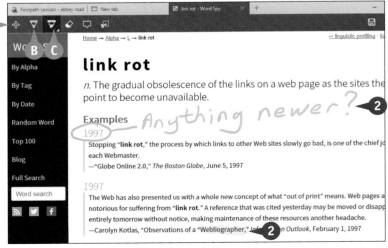

Add a Typed Note

1. Click **Add a typed note** (🖼️).

2. Click the web page where you want the note to appear.

3. Type your note.

4. Click outside the text box.

Ⓓ You can click the typed note number to redisplay the text.

Save Your Web Notes

1. Click **Save Web Note** (🖫).

2. Edit the note name, as needed.

3. Select a location.

4. Click **Add**.

 Microsoft Edge saves your web note to the Quick Notes section of the OneNote app.

5. Click **Exit**.

TIPS

How do I display a saved Web Note?

Microsoft Edge stores your saved Web Notes as favorites, so to display a saved Web Note, click **Hub** (≡), click **Favorites** (☆), and then click the saved note.

What is a web page clip?

A *clip* is a rectangular section of the web page that you can copy and then paste to another program, such as OneNote or Paint. To copy a clip, display the Web Note tools and then click **Clip** (🖼️). Click and drag a rectangle over the area you want to save. When you release, Edge automatically copies the area.

Search for Sites

I f you need information on a specific topic, Microsoft Edge has a built-in feature that enables you to quickly search the web for sites that have the information you require. The web has a number of sites called *search engines* that enable you to find what you are looking for. By default, Microsoft Edge uses the Bing search site. You use the Microsoft Edge address bar to enter a word or phrase that is representative of the information that you seek. Microsoft Edge passes the word or phrase to Bing, which then looks for pages that match your text.

Search for Sites

1 Click inside the address bar.

Microsoft Edge selects the current address.

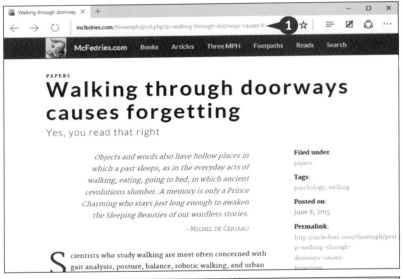

2 Type a word, phrase, or question that represents the information you want to find.

3 Press Enter.

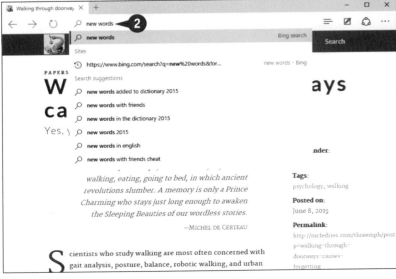

Ⓐ A list of pages that match your search text appears.

④ Click a web page.

The page appears.

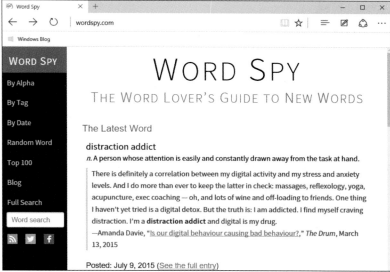

How can I get better search results?

Simple, one-word searches often return tens of thousands of *hits,* or matching sites. To improve your searching, type multiple search terms that define what you are looking for. To search for an exact phrase, enclose the words in quotation marks. If you want to find a page that includes one term or another, separate the two terms with the word OR (in capitals). If you want the results to exclude pages that contain a particular term, precede that term with a minus sign (–).

Download a File

Many websites make files available for you to use on your computer, so you need to know how to save them to your PC, a process known as *downloading*. After you have downloaded a file, you can open it on your computer as long as you have an app that can work with the type of file you downloaded. For example, if the file is an Excel workbook, you need either Excel or a compatible program. You can either open the downloaded file right away, or open it later by displaying your downloaded files.

Download a File

Download and Open a File

1 Navigate to the page that contains the link to the file.

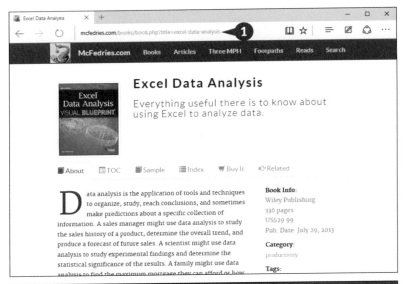

2 Click the link to the file.

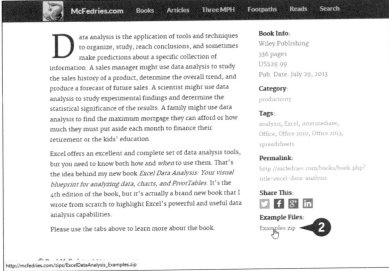

Microsoft Edge downloads the file to your PC and displays the Information bar.

③ Click **Open**.

Ⓐ If you do not want to work with the file right away, you can click **Close** (✕), instead.

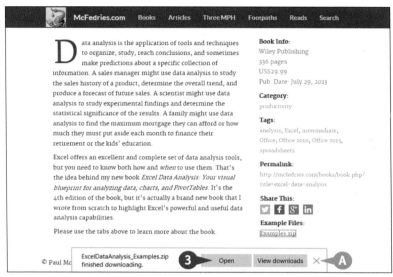

View Your Downloaded Files

① Click **Hub** (≡).

② Click **Downloads** (↓).

Note: If you have just downloaded a file, you can also click **View downloads** in the Information bar.

Microsoft Edge displays the Downloads list.

Is it safe to download files from the web?

Yes, as long as you only download files from sites you trust. If you ever notice that Microsoft Edge is attempting to download a file without your permission, cancel the download immediately because it is likely that the file contains a virus or other malware.

If you do not completely trust a file that you have downloaded, use an antivirus program, such as Microsoft Security Essentials (http://windows.microsoft.com/en-us/windows/security-essentials-download), Avast! Antivirus (www.avast.com), or AVG Internet Security (http://free.avg.com) to scan the file before you open it.

Sending and Receiving Email

You can use the Mail app to work with your email account. You can use Mail to send email messages and file attachments. You can also use Mail to receive and read incoming messages.

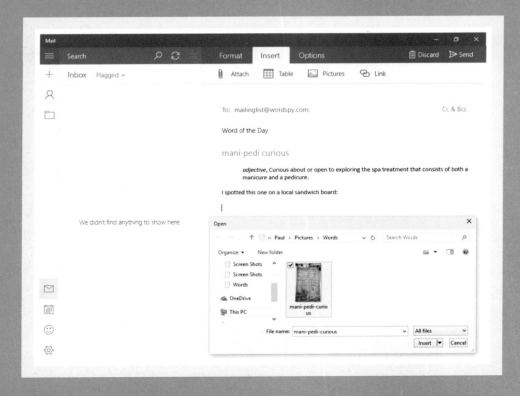

Configure an Email Account

Before you can send an email message, you must add your email account to the Mail application. This also enables you to use Mail to retrieve the messages that others have sent to your account.

You use Mail to set up web-based email accounts with services such as Hotmail and Gmail. Note, however, that if you are already signing in to Windows using a Microsoft account, then Windows automatically adds that account to the Mail app — so you need to follow the steps in this section only if you want to add another account to Mail.

Configure an Email Account

① On the Start menu, click **Mail** (not shown).

Mail opens.

Note: If you are starting Mail for the first time and the app prompts you to add an account, skip to step **4**.

② Click **Settings** (⚙).

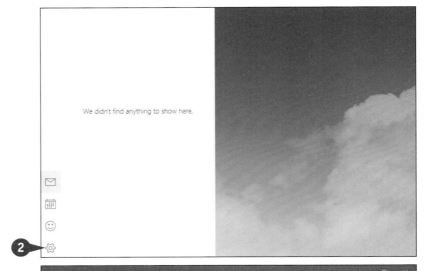

The Settings pane appears.

③ Click **Accounts**.

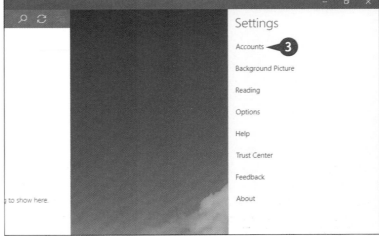

The Accounts pane appears.

④ Click **Add account**.

The Choose an Account menu appears.

⑤ Click the type of account that you want to add.

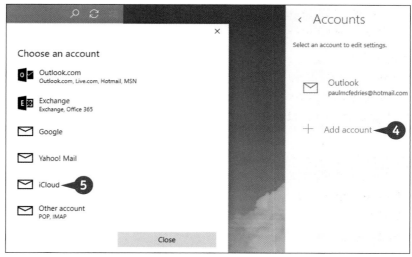

Mail asks for your account email address and password.

⑥ Type your email address.

⑦ Type your email password.

⑧ Click **Sign in**.

Mail adds your email account to the Accounts pane.

How do I add my Exchange account to Mail?
You will need to obtain from your Exchange administrator or provider the account's server address, domain name, and username — and you will need to know your account's email address and password, of course. In many cases, you can follow steps **1** to **4**. Click **Exchange** and follow steps **6** to **8**. If Mail cannot find your settings, enter your Exchange domain name and click **Sign in**. If Mail still cannot locate your account, click **Advanced**, enter the server address, and then click **Sign in**.

Send an Email Message

If you know the email address of a person or organization, you can send an email message to that address. Each address uniquely identifies the location of an Internet mailbox. An address takes the form *username@domain*, where *username* is the name of the person's account, and *domain* is the Internet name of the company that provides the person's email account.

When you send an email message, it travels through your email provider's outgoing mail server. This server routes the message to the recipient's incoming mail server, which then stores the message in the recipient's mailbox.

Send an Email Message

① In Mail, click **New mail** (+).

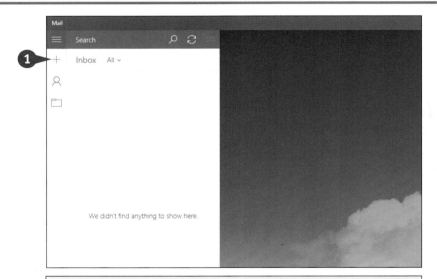

A message window appears.

② Type the email address of the recipient.

Ⓐ To send a copy of the message to another person, click **Cc & Bcc**, and then type that person's email address in the Cc field.

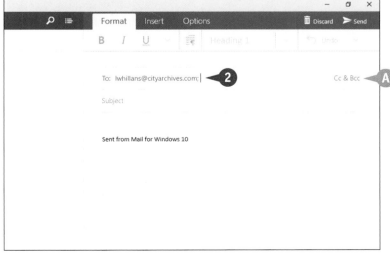

3 Type a subject for the message.

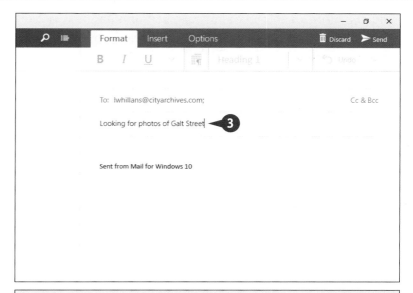

4 Type the message.

Note: See the next section, "Format the Message Text," to learn how to apply formatting to your message.

5 Click **Send**.

Mail sends your message.

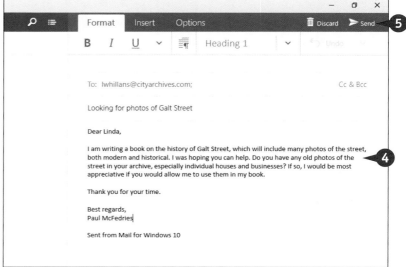

Format the Message Text

You can add visual interest and make your message easier to read by formatting your message text. A plain email message is quick to compose, but it is often worth the extra time to add formatting to your text. For example, you can add bold or italic formatting to highlight a word or phrase. Mail supports a wide range of formatting options, including font colors, highlights, emoticons, bulleted lists, and numbered lists. All these formatting options have their place, but be careful not to overdo it, or you may make your message *harder* to read.

Format the Message Text

Format the Message Font

1. Select the text that you want to format.

2. Click the font formatting that you want to apply, such as **Bold** (**B**), **Italic** (***I***), or **Underline** (**U**).

Ⓐ For more font options, click **⌄**.

Mail applies the font formatting to the text.

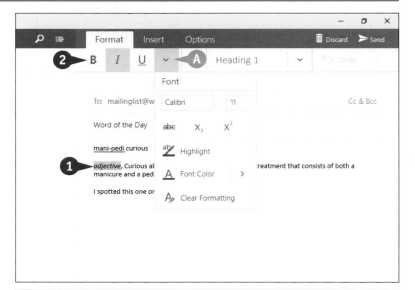

Format a Message Paragraph

1. Select the paragraph that you want to format.

2. Click **Paragraph** (☰).

3. Click the paragraph formatting that you want to apply, such as Bullets, Numbering, Indents, or Alignment.

Mail applies the paragraph formatting to the text.

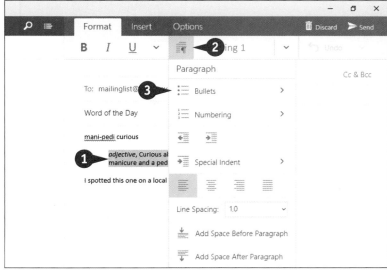

Apply a Style

1 Select the text that you want to format.

2 Click the Styles ⌄.

3 Click a style.

Mail applies the style to the text.

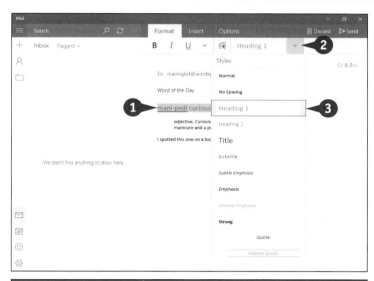

Insert a Picture

1 Position the cursor where you want the picture to appear.

2 Click the **Insert** tab.

3 Click **Pictures**.

The Open dialog box appears.

4 Select the location of the picture.

5 Click the picture.

6 Click **Insert**.

Mail adds the picture to the email message.

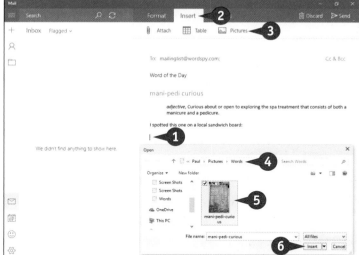

TIPS

Can I make adjustments to a picture that I have inserted in my email message?

Yes. Click the picture and then click the **Picture** tab. Click **Rotate** to rotate the image, or **Crop** to crop unwanted portions of the image. You can use the sizing handles that appear around the image to adjust its size. If you are not happy with the new image dimensions, click the image, click the **Picture** tab, and then click **Reset Size**.

How do I set the message priority?

Setting the priority level of your message helps the recipient know how to handle your message. Click the **Options** tab and then click **High importance** (!) or **Low importance** (↓).

Add a File Attachment

I f you have a document that you want to send to another person, you can attach the document to an email message. A typical email message is fine for short notes, but you may have something more complex to communicate, such as budget numbers or a slide show, or some form of media that you want to share, such as an image or a song. Because these more complex types of data usually come in a separate file — such as a spreadsheet, presentation file, or video file — it makes sense to send that file to your recipient as an attachment.

Add a File Attachment

1 Click the **Insert** tab.

2 Click **Attach**.

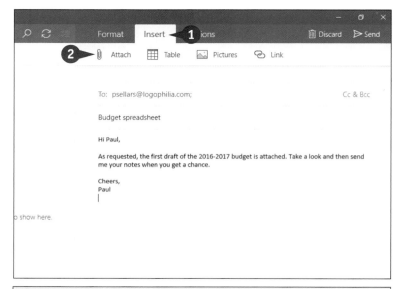

The Open dialog box appears.

3 Select the folder that contains the file you want to attach.

④ Click the file that you want to attach.

⑤ Click **Open**.

Ⓐ Mail attaches the file to the message.

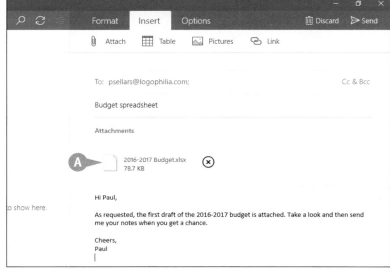

Is there a limit to the number of files that I can attach to a message?
There is no practical limit to the number of files that you can attach to a message. However, you should be careful with the total *size* of the files that you send. If you or the recipient has a slow Internet connection, sending or receiving the message can take an extremely long time. Also, many Internet service providers (ISPs) place a limit on the size of a message's attachments, which is usually between 2MB and 10MB. In general, use email to send only a few small files at a time.

Save a Draft of a Message

If you cannot complete or send your message right away, you can save it as a draft and open it again later. As you work on an email message, you might find that you need to give it more thought or that you have to do more research. Rather than discard your work, you can close the message and Mail will save it for you automatically. Mail stores the saved message in your account's Drafts folder. When you are ready to resume editing the message, you can open it from the Drafts folder.

Save a Draft of a Message

Save the Draft

1 Compose the message up to the point where you want Mail to save it.

2 Click elsewhere in the Mail window, such as an Inbox message.

A Alternatively, you can click **All Folders** (🗀) and then click a folder.

Mail saves the message to your Drafts folder.

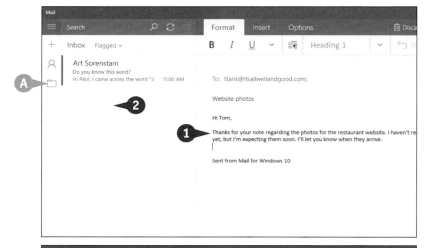

Open the Draft

1 Click **All Folders** (🗀).

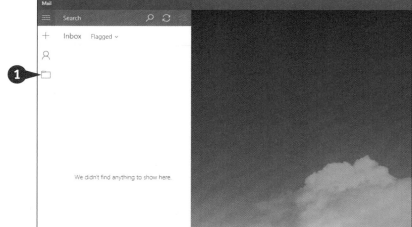

Mail displays your account folders.

2 Click **Drafts**.

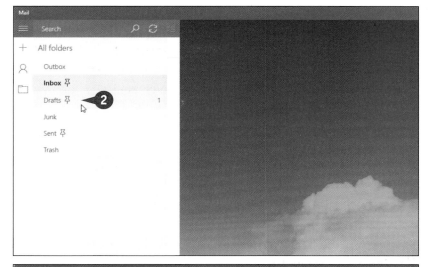

3 Click the draft that you want to open.

Mail opens the message for editing.

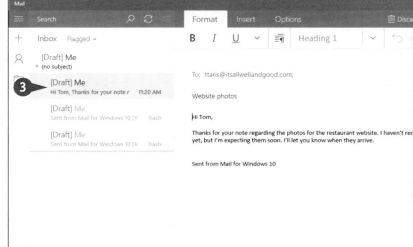

TIP

What are the other account folders used for?

Sent	Holds copies of outgoing messages that you have sent.	Junk	Holds incoming messages that Mail has deemed to be unsolicited commercial emails, also known as *junk mail* or *spam*.
Outbox	Holds outgoing messages that are in the process of being sent.	Trash	Holds messages that you have deleted from other folders.

Receive and Read Email Messages

When another person sends you an email message, that message ends up in your email account's mailbox on the incoming mail server maintained by your ISP or email provider. However, that company does not automatically pass along that message to you. Instead, you must use Mail to connect to your mailbox on the incoming mail server and then retrieve any messages waiting for you. By default, Mail automatically retrieves new messages as they arrive, but you can also check for new messages at any time.

Receive and Read Email Messages

Receive Email Messages

1 Click **Refresh** ().

Mail checks for new messages.

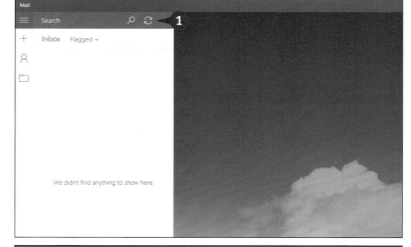

Ⓐ If you have new messages, they appear in your Inbox folder.

Ⓑ This bar appears beside messages that you have not yet read.

Ⓒ The symbol means that the message has an attachment.

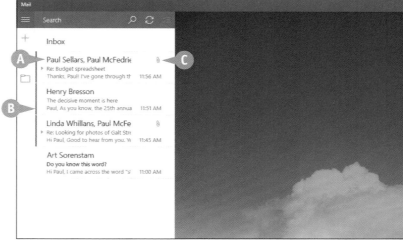

Read a Message

1 Click the message.

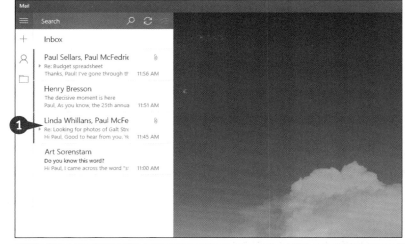

The message text appears in the preview pane.

2 Read the message text.

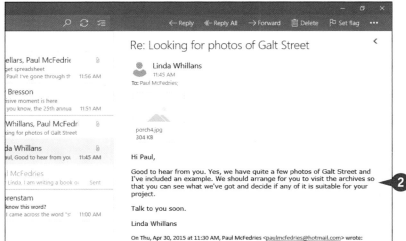

Why do new messages sometimes appear in my Inbox when I have not clicked Sync?
For certain types of accounts, Mail supports a feature called *push* that can send new messages to your Inbox automatically. In this case, when the mail server receives a new message, it immediately sends the message to your Inbox without your having to run the Sync command. Note that this feature works if you are using a Hotmail, Live.com, or Outlook.com email account, as well as a Gmail account.

Reply to a Message

When a message you receive requires some kind of response — whether it is answering a question, supplying information, or providing comments — you can reply to that message. Most replies go only to the person who sent the original message. However, you can also send the reply to all the people who were included in the original message's To and Cc lines. Mail includes the text of the original message in the reply, but you might want to edit the original message text to include only enough of the original message to put your reply into context.

Reply to a Message

1 Click the message to which you want to reply.

2 Click **Reply**.

Ⓐ If you prefer to respond to all the message recipients, click **Reply All** instead.

Note: See the first Tip for more information.

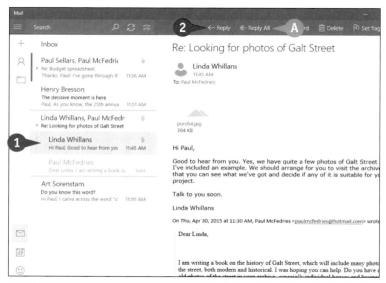

A message window appears.

Ⓑ Mail automatically inserts the sender of the original message as the recipient.

Ⓒ Mail also inserts the subject line, preceded by "RE:."

Ⓓ Mail includes the original message's addresses (To and From), date, subject, and text at the bottom of the reply.

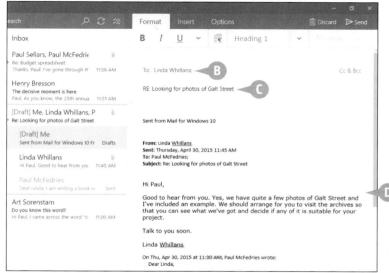

3 Edit the original message to include only the text relevant to your reply.

4 Click the area above the original message text.

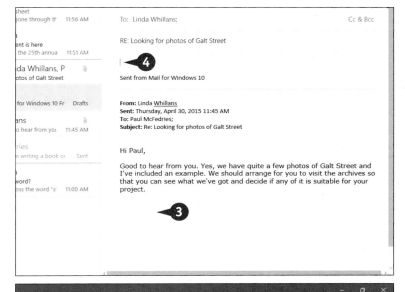

5 Type your reply.

6 Click **Send**.

Mail sends your reply.

Note: Mail stores a copy of your reply in the Sent folder.

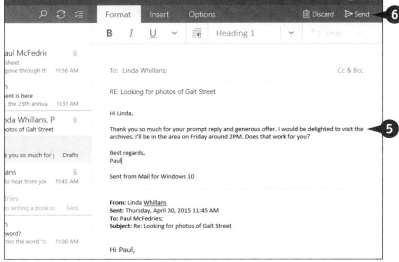

TIPS

What is the difference between Reply and Reply All?
You can click **Reply** to respond only to the person who sent the message, or click **Reply all** to respond to the sender as well as any other addresses that the sender included in the original message's To and Cc fields.

Should I edit the original message text in my reply?
If the original message is short, you usually do not need to edit the text. However, if the original message is long, and your response deals only with part of that message, you will save the recipient time by deleting everything except the relevant portion of the text.

Forward a Message

If a message has information that is relevant to or concerns another person, you can forward a copy of the message to that person. You can also include your own comments in the forward.

In the body of the forward, Mail includes the original message's addresses, date, and subject line. Below this information, Mail also includes the text of the original message. In most cases, you will leave the entire message intact so that your recipient can see it. However, if only part of the message is relevant to the recipient, you should edit the original message accordingly.

Forward a Message

1 Click the message that you want to forward.

2 Click **Forward**.

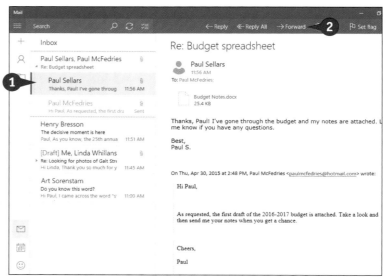

A message window appears.

Ⓐ Mail inserts the subject line, preceded by "FW:."

Ⓑ The original message's addresses (To and From), date, subject, attachments, and text are included.

3 Select or type the email address of the person to whom you are forwarding the message.

Ⓒ To send a copy of the message to another person, click **Cc & Bcc**, and then enter that person's email address in the Cc field.

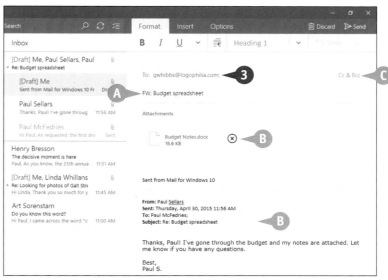

④ If necessary, edit the original message to include only the text relevant to your forward.

⑤ Click the area above the original message text.

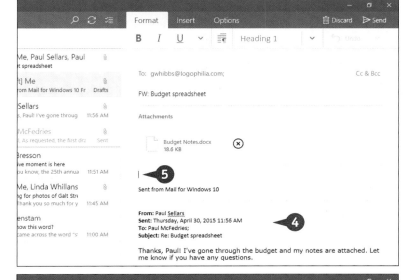

⑥ Type your comments.

⑦ Click **Send**.

Mail sends your forward.

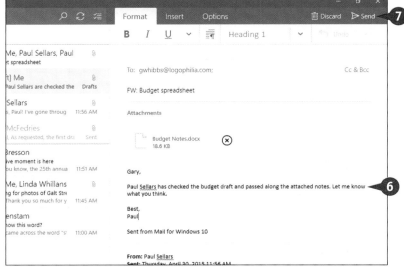

How do I view the text of a forward or reply after I have sent it?

When you send a forward or a reply (or an original message), Mail stores a copy of the message in the Sent folder. To view the message, click **All Folders** (⌐) to display the All Folders list and then click **Sent**.

When I forward a message, is it possible to not include an attachment that came with the message?

Yes. After you click the message and then click **Forward**, the message attachment appears by default as part of the forwarded message. This is usually what you want, but you can remove the attachment by clicking **Remove** (⊗).

Open and Save an Attachment

When a message comes in and displays the attachment symbol (a paper clip), it means that the sender has included a file as an attachment to the message. If you just want to take a quick look at the file, you can open the attachment directly from Mail. Alternatively, if you want to keep a copy of the file on your computer, you can save the attachment to your hard drive.

Be careful when dealing with attached files. Computer viruses are often transmitted by email attachments.

Open and Save an Attachment

Open an Attachment

1. Click the message that has the attachment, as indicated by a paper clip (📎).

A. A list of the message attachments appears.

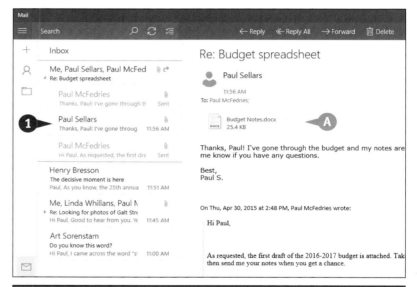

2. Click the attachment that you want to open.

 The file opens in the appropriate program.

Note: Instead of opening the file, you may see a message that says, "Windows can't open this type of file." This means that you need to install the appropriate program for the type of file. If you are not sure, ask the person who sent you the file what program you need.

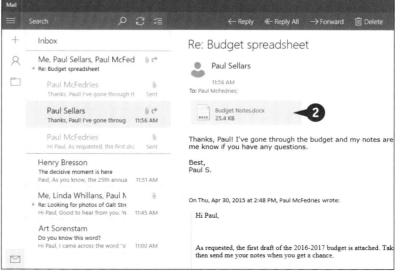

Save an Attachment

1 Click the message that has the attachment, as indicated by a paper clip (📎).

B A list of the message attachments appears.

2 Right-click the attachment that you want to save.

3 Click **Save**.

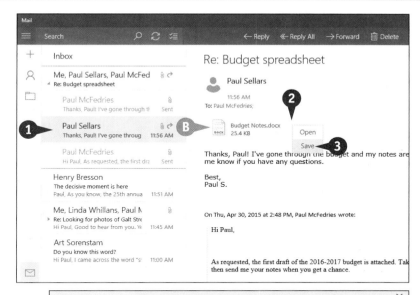

The Save As dialog box appears.

4 Click the folder where you want to store the file.

5 Edit the filename, if needed.

6 Click **Save**.

Mail saves the attachment to your PC's hard drive.

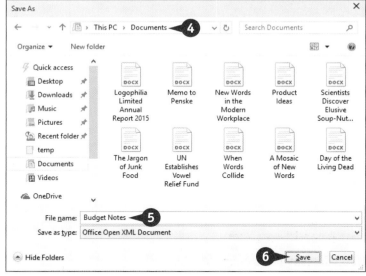

Why must I be careful when working with email attachments?

Email attachments are the most common way that nefarious users attempt to infect PCs with viruses and other malware. When you open such an attachment, the virus infects your computer and then, without your knowledge, uses your email program and your address book to send messages with more copies of itself attached. The nastier versions also mess with your computer by deleting data or corrupting files. Never open an attachment that comes from someone you do not know. If someone you know sends you an attachment unexpectedly, write that person back and confirm that he or she really did send the file.

Delete a Message

After you have used Mail for a while, you may find that you have a lot of messages in your Inbox folder. The more messages you have, the harder it becomes to find a message that you want and the more time-consuming it gets to navigate the messages. To keep the Inbox uncluttered and easier to navigate, you should delete any messages that you have already read and do not need to keep.

Note that when you delete a message, Mail actually sends it to the Trash folder. If you delete a message accidentally, you can retrieve it from the Trash folder.

Delete a Message

Delete a Message from the Inbox

1 Click the message that you want to delete.

2 Click **Delete**.

Note: If you have a tablet PC, you can also delete a message by swiping to the left across the message.

Mail removes the message from the Inbox and moves it to the Trash folder.

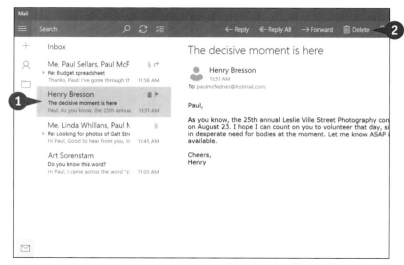

Restore a Deleted Message

1 Click **All Folders** ().

Mail displays the folders list.

2 Click **Trash**.

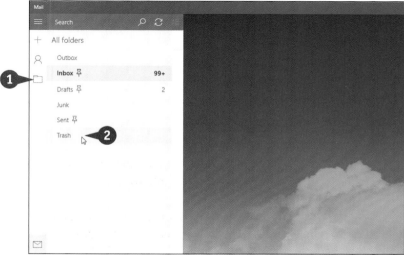

Mail opens the Trash folder.

3 Right-click the message that you want to restore.

4 Click **Move**.

Mail displays a list of folders.

5 Click **Inbox**.

Mail restores the message to the Inbox folder.

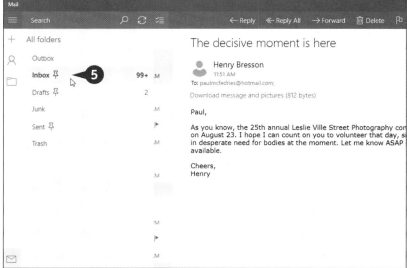

TIP

Can I remove a message permanently?
Yes, as long as you are sure you will never need to work with the message again, you can delete it permanently from your account. However, this operation is not reversible, so you really need to be certain that you no longer need the message.

Follow steps **1** and **2** to open the Trash folder, right-click the message you want to remove, and then click **Delete**. Mail removes the message permanently from your account.

Create a Folder for Saving Messages

After you have used Mail for a while, you may find that you have a lot of messages in your Inbox folder. To keep the Inbox uncluttered, you can create new folders and then move messages from the Inbox to the new folders.

To help keep your messages organized, you should use each folder you create to save related messages. For example, you could create separate folders for people you correspond with regularly, projects you are working on, different work departments, and so on. By saving each message to the appropriate folder, you make it easier to find your messages in the future.

Create a Folder for Saving Messages

Create a Folder

1 Use a web browser to navigate to http://mail.live.com and sign in to your account.

2 Click **New folder**.

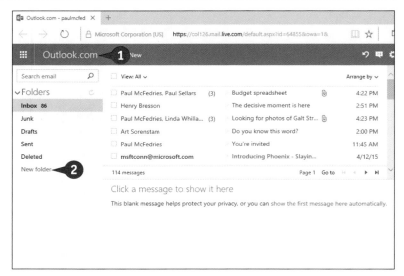

You are prompted to enter the folder name.

3 Type the name of the new folder.

4 Press Enter or click outside the text box.

The new folder is created.

Note: It might take a few minutes before the new folder appears in the Mail app.

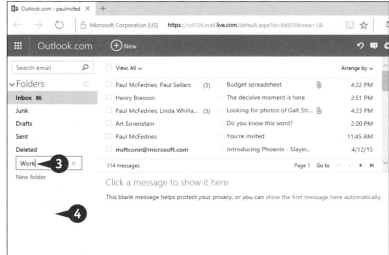

Move a Message to Another Folder

1 In Mail, right-click the message you want to move.

2 Click **Move**.

Mail displays the list of folders.

3 Click the folder you want to use as the destination.

Mail moves the message.

How do I rename a folder?

Use a web browser to sign in to your account. In the Folders list, right-click the folder you want to rename and then click **Rename**. In the text box, type the new name and then either press Enter or click outside the text box. You can rename only folders that you have created.

How do I delete a folder?

Use a web browser to sign in to your account. In the Folders list, right-click the folder you want to remove and then click **Delete**. You can delete only folders that you have created. When you delete a folder, you also delete any messages stored in that folder.

Configure Mail Options

The Mail app comes with a few options that you can configure to make the program suit the way you prefer to work. Several of these options are related to how you use swipe gestures in the Mail app, if you are running Windows on a touch PC or tablet. You can also configure the Mail app background image and whether the app displays notifications. Finally, you can also customize the signature text that appears in the body of the messages you create as well as the replies and forwards you send.

Configure Mail Options

1 Click **Settings** (⚙).

The Settings pane appears.

2 To change the Mail app background image, click **Background Picture**.

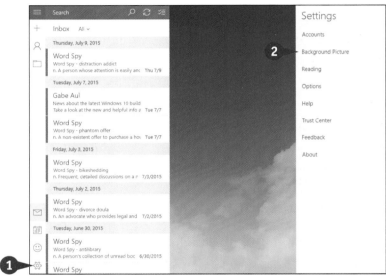

Mail displays the Background Picture pane.

3 Click **Browse**.

The Open dialog box appears.

The Open dialog box appears.

4 Click the image.

5 Click **Open**.

6 Click **Back** ⟨ to return to the Settings pane.

7 Click **Reading** (not shown).

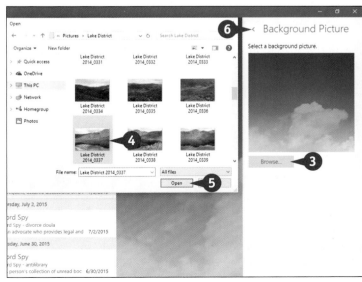

The Reading pane appears.

8 If you click the **Auto-open next item** switch to **On**, Mail automatically opens the next message after you use a swipe gesture to delete a message.

9 In the Mark Item as Read section, click an option to specify when Mail marks a message as having been read (○ changes to ●).

10 Click **Back** ‹ to return to the Settings pane.

11 Click **Options** (not shown)

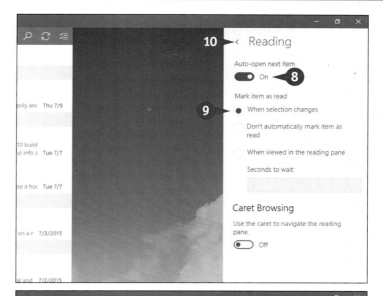

The Options pane appears.

12 If you do not want to use gestures on a tablet, click the **Swipe actions** switch to **Off**.

13 Click the **Swipe right / hover** ∨ and select the action that Mail performs when you swipe right on a message.

14 Click the **Swipe left / hover** ∨ and select the action that Mail performs when you swipe left on a message.

15 To use a signature, click the **Use an email signature** switch to **On**.

16 Edit the signature text here.

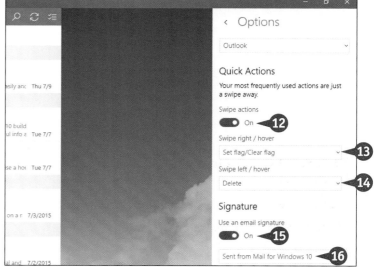

TIPS

What is a flag?

A *flag* is an indicator that you can add to a message by clicking the message and then clicking **Flag**. Mail adds a flag icon (⚑) to the message, which serves as a visual reminder. This is useful if you need a prompt to follow up with a message or to perform some other action based on that message.

What is a signature?

A *signature* is a snippet of text that appears at the bottom of any message that you send, including original messages, replies, and forwards. Most signatures offer information about the sender, such as contact data, work information, or even a short quotation or saying.

Getting Social with Windows

You can use Windows to manage your social schedule. You can use the People app to store contact information, connect to social networks, and keep track of friends. You can use the Calendar app to schedule meetings, appointments, and other events.

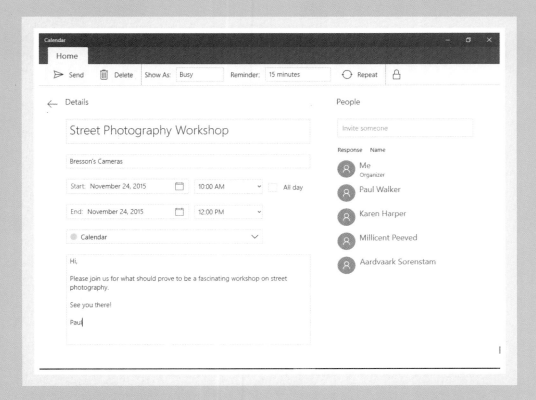

Create a Contact

You can easily store information about your friends, family, and colleagues, as well as send messages to them, by using the People app to create a contact for each person. Each contact can store a wide variety of information, such as a person's first and last names, company name, email address, phone number, and street address.

If you already have contacts on a social network such as Facebook or LinkedIn, you do not need to enter those contacts manually. Instead, you can connect your social network account to your Microsoft account, as described in the next few sections.

Create a Contact

1 In the taskbar's Search box, type **people**.

2 Click **People**.

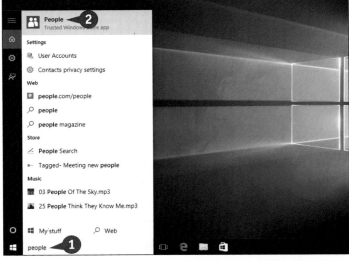

The People app loads.

3 Click **Add contact** (+).

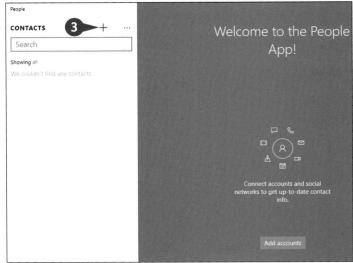

The New Contact screen appears.

4 Type the contact's name.

5 Click the **Phone** ∨ and then click the type of phone number that you want to enter.

6 Type the contact's phone number.

A You can click **Add** (＋) to add another phone number.

7 Click the **Email** ∨ and then click the type of email address that you want to enter.

8 Type the contact's email address.

B You can click the **Email** ＋ to add another email address.

9 Click **Save** (💾).

The People app creates the new contact.

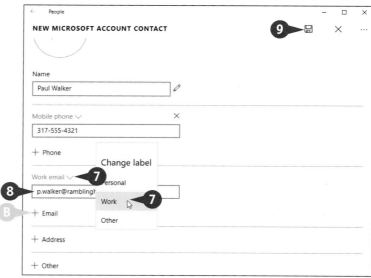

Is there an easy way to send an email to a contact?
Yes. Normally, you would use the Mail app, as described in Chapter 4. If you are already working in the People app, however, it is easier to click the person's entry in the Contacts list to open the contact and then click the **Email** address you want to use.

How do I record a contact's physical address?
With the new contact open for editing, click the **Address** ＋ and then click the label you want for the address. In the text boxes that appear, type the contact's Street address, City, State/province, Zip/postal code, and Country/region.

Add Your Google Account

You can add your Google account to Windows to access your Google contacts (as well as your Google calendar and email) from your Windows computer. To do so, you must provide Windows with your Google account login data.

After you have added your Google account, you can use the People app to view your Google contacts. You can use the Calendar app to view your Google events and appointments, and you can use the Mail app to view your Gmail messages.

Add Your Google Account

1 In the People app, click **More** (⋯).

2 Click **Settings**.

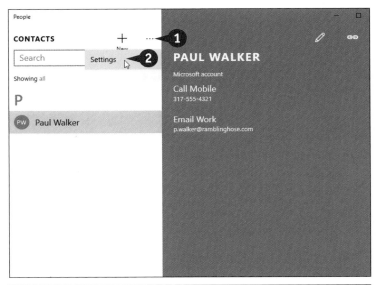

The Settings screen appears.

3 Click **Add an account**.

4 Click **Google**.

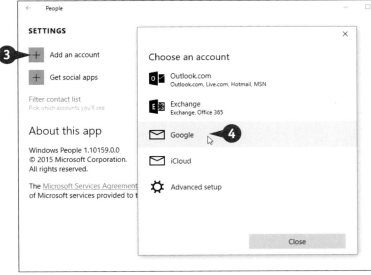

The People app prompts you for your Google login data.

5 Type your Google email address.

6 Click **Next**.

7 Type your Google password.

8 Click **Sign in**.

The People app shows you what it will do with your Google data.

9 Click **Accept**.

Windows connects your Google account to your Microsoft account.

10 Click **Done** (not shown).

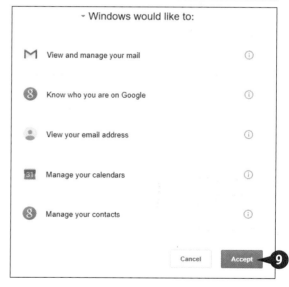

Can I control what type of Google content appears in Windows?
Yes, you can configure the type of content to sync between Google and Windows and how often that content syncs. In the People app, click **More** (⋯), click **Settings**, click **Gmail**, and then click **Change mailbox sync settings**. People displays the Gmail Sync Settings dialog box. Click the **Sync contacts and calendars** ⌄ and then click how often you want Windows to sync your Google data. In the Sync Options group, use the **Email**, **Calendar**, and **Contacts** switches to toggle each type of content on or off.

Add Your iCloud Account

You can add your iCloud account to Windows to access your iCloud contacts (as well as your iCloud calendar and email) from your Windows computer. To do so, you must provide Windows with your iCloud account login data.

After you have added your iCloud account, you can use the People app to view your iCloud contacts. You can use the Calendar app to view your iCloud events and appointments, and you can use the Mail app to view your iCloud messages.

Add Your iCloud Account

1 In the People app, click **More** (⋯).

2 Click **Settings**.

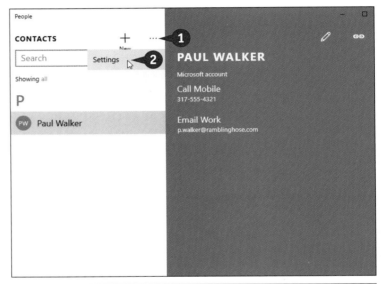

The Settings screen appears.

3 Click **Add an account**.

4 Click **iCloud**.

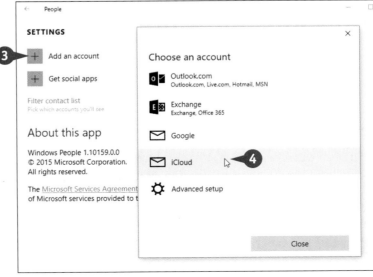

The People app prompts you for your iCloud login data.

5 Type your iCloud email address.

6 Type your iCloud password.

7 Click **Sign-in**.

People prompts you to enter your name.

8 Type the name you would like to associate with your iCloud account.

9 Click **Sign-in**.

Windows connects your iCloud account to your Microsoft account.

10 Click **Done**.

 TIP

Can I control what type of iCloud content appears in Windows?
Yes, you can configure the type of content to sync between iCloud and Windows and how often that content syncs. In the People app, click **More** (⋯), click **Settings**, click **iCloud**, and then click **Change mailbox sync settings**. People displays the iCloud Sync Settings dialog box. Click the **Sync contacts and calendars** ⌄ and then click how often you want Windows to sync your iCloud data. In the Sync Options group, use the **Email**, **Calendar**, and **Contacts** switches to toggle each type of content on or off.

View a Contact

After you have added contacts and connected your other accounts to Windows, you can use the People app to view your contacts. The information that you see when you view a contact depends on how the contact was added to Windows. If you added the contact yourself, you see the information that you entered. If the contact was added by connecting another account to Windows, you see the data provided by that account. If you have many contacts, you can also use the People app's Search feature to locate the contact you want to view.

View a Contact

View a Contact

1 In the People app, scroll the Contacts list up or down to locate the contact you want to view.

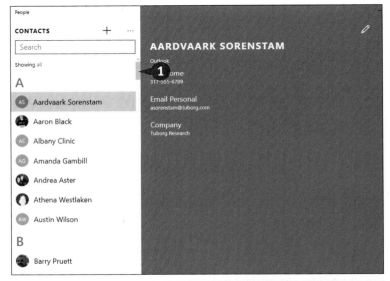

2 Click the contact.

A The People app displays the contact's data.

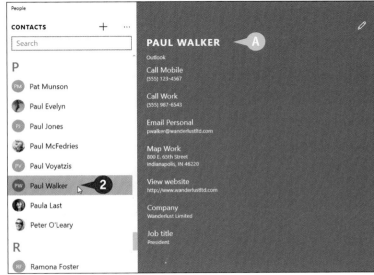

Search for a Contact

1 Click in the People app's Search box.

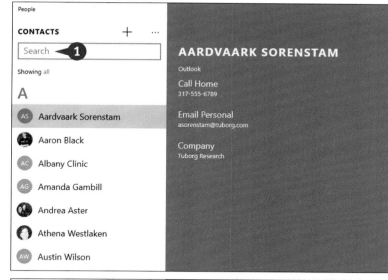

2 Begin typing the name of the contact you want to view.

B People displays a list of contacts with names that match your typing.

3 When you see the contact you want to view, click the name in the search results.

The People app saves the updated data.

Is there an easier way to navigate the Contacts list?
Yes. Click any of the letters that the People app uses to divide the Contacts list alphabetically. This converts the Contacts list to a grid of letters and you then click the letter you want to view.

How do I delete a contact?
If you no longer need a contact, you should delete it from the People app to reduce clutter in the Contacts list. First, use either of the techniques outlined in this section to locate the contact you want to remove. Right-click the contact and then click **Delete**. When the People app asks you to confirm, click **Delete**.

Edit a Contact

If you need to make changes to the information already in a contact, or if you need to add new information to a contact, you can edit the contact from within the People app. While editing a contact, you can modify the existing information, add new information to the contact, or delete existing information.

Edit a Contact

1 In the People app, click the contact you want to edit.

2 Click **Edit** (✏️).

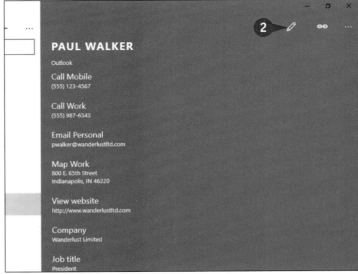

People makes the contact's fields available for editing.

3 Edit the existing fields as required.

4 To add a field, click the + beside the field type you want to use and then type the data.

5 To remove a field, move the mouse ⌖ over the field and then click **Remove** (✕).

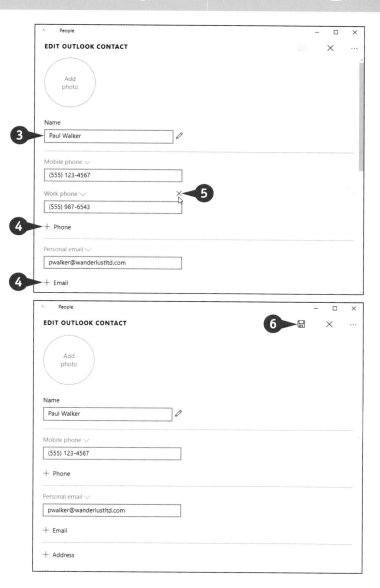

6 When you complete your edits, click **Save** (🖫).

People saves the edited contact.

TIP

Can I add other more detailed name data for a contact?
Yes, the People app offers multiple name fields: First Name, Last Name, Middle Name, Nickname, Title, Suffix, Phonetic First Name, and Phonetic Last Name. To specify any of this data, follow steps **1** and **2** to open the contact for editing, and then click **Edit** (✎) beside the Name field. In the Edit Name dialog box that appears, fill in the name fields as needed and then click **Done**.

Assign a Photo to a Contact

You can add visual interest to the People app and make it more useful by assigning photos to your contacts. By default, the People app shows a standard image for each contact. For your Microsoft account, that image is a generic headshot, but other accounts have different images. For example, Google's images consist of just the contact's initials. Assigning photos not only improves the look of the People app, but it also helps you remember your contacts, particularly if they are business colleagues or similar acquaintances that you do not see very often.

Assign a Photo to a Contact

1 In the People app, click the contact you want to work with.

2 Click **Edit** (✎).

People opens the contact for editing.

3 Click **Add photo**.

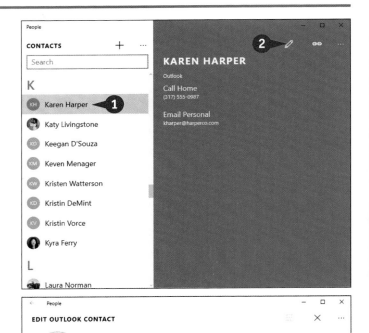

A version of the Photos app displays your photos.

④ Click the photo you want to add.

People prompts you to choose the area of the photo that you want to use for the contact.

⑤ Click and drag the photo to set the area you want to use within the circle.

⑥ Click and drag any of the four handles to set the size of the circle.

⑦ Click **Apply** (✓).

People adds the photo to the contact.

⑧ Click **Save** (🖫).

People saves the edited contact.

How do I change a contact's photo?
Follow steps **1** and **2** to open the contact for editing, and then click the existing photo to open the Photos app and see your photos. Click the new photo you want to use and then follow steps **5** to **8** to set the photo position and size and save your changes.

How do I remove a contact's photo?
If you no longer want to use a photo for a contact, you can delete it. Follow steps **1** and **2** to open the contact for editing. Right-click the existing photo and then click **Delete photo**. People removes the photo from the contact. Click **Save** (🖫) to preserve your changes.

Add Extra Fields to a Contact

The People app offers several other fields that you can add to a contact to store more data about that person or company. The default editing screen shows only a few field types: Name, Phone, Email, and Address. However, People also supports many other field types that enable you to store data such as the contact's website address, company name, job title, and office location. You can also save personal data such as the name of the contact's significant other and the contact's birthday and anniversary. Finally, you can also add a Notes field to hold any other required data.

Add Extra Fields to a Contact

1 In the People app, click the contact you want to edit.

2 Click **Edit** (✏).

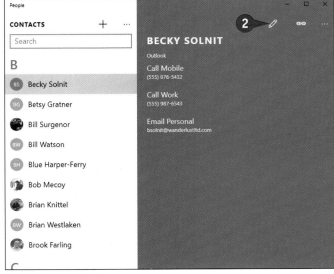

People makes the contact's fields available for editing.

3 Click the **Other** ╋.

4 Click the type of field you want to add.

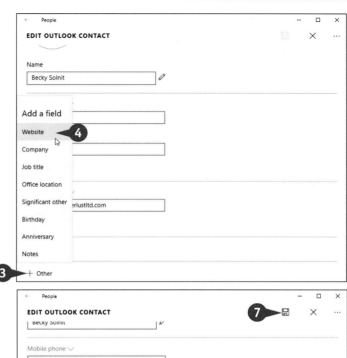

5 Fill in the data for the new field.

6 Repeat steps **3** to **5** to add extra fields as needed.

7 When you complete your edits, click **Save** (💾).

People saves the edited contact.

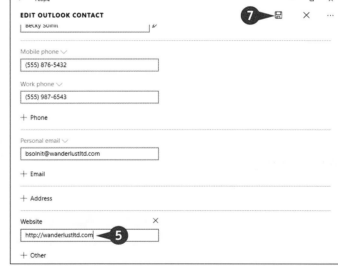

Is there a way to add a contact's website without having to memorize a long address?
Yes, you can copy the address from the Microsoft Edge web browser. In the taskbar, click **Microsoft Edge** (🔲) and then navigate to the contact's website. In the address bar, right-click the address, click **Select All**, and then either press Ctrl+C or right-click the selected address and then click **Copy**. Switch to the People app, follow steps **1** to **4** to add the Website field, click inside the field, and then either press Ctrl+V or right-click the field and then click **Paste**.

Filter the Contacts List

You can make a long Contacts list easier to navigate and manage by filtering it to hide certain contacts. For example, if you mostly use People to locate contacts for phone calling or text messaging, you can filter the Contacts list to hide all those contacts who do not have a phone number. Similarly, if you have multiple accounts added to the People app, you might find that this creates many duplicate entries. You can fix this problem by filtering the Contacts list to hide all contacts from a particular account.

Filter the Contacts List

Hide Contacts Without Phone Numbers

1 In the People app, scroll to the top of the Contacts list.

2 Click **all**.

The Filter Contacts dialog box appears.

3 Click the **Hide contacts without phone numbers** switch to **On**.

4 Click **Done**.

People only shows those contacts who have at least one phone number.

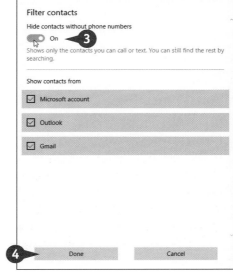

Hide Contacts by Account

1 In the People app, scroll to the top of the Contacts list.

2 Click **all**.

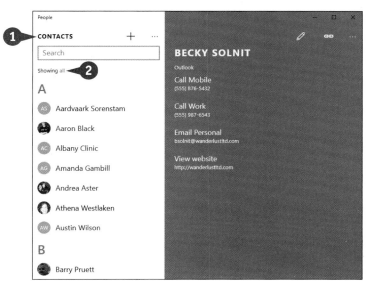

The Filter Contacts dialog box appears.

3 Click the account you want to hide (☑ changes to ☐).

4 Click **Done**.

People hides the contacts from the account you deselected in step **3**.

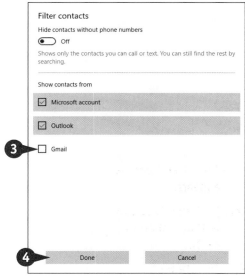

How do I remove an account from the People app?

If you find that you do not use the contacts from a particular account, or if a particular account contains all or mostly duplicate contacts of another account, you might prefer to remove that account entirely rather than just hiding it. Note, however, that removing an account also removes that account's email from the mail app and its calendars from the Calendar app.

If you still prefer to remove the account, click **More** (···) and then click **Settings**. Click the account you want to remove and then click **Delete account**. When People asks you to confirm, click **Delete**.

Link Multiple Profiles for a Contact

ou can make your Contacts list more manageable and more useful by linking two or more contacts that are profiles of the same person. When you add multiple accounts to the People app, you might end up with the same contact listed two or more times. If those profiles contain different data — for example, one might contain personal information while the other contains work information — it is a hassle to try to remember which is which. A better alternative is to link those profiles, which tells People to display all the contact's data in a single profile.

Link Multiple Profiles for a Contact

1 In the People app, click one of the profiles that you want to link.

2 Click **Link** (⚭).

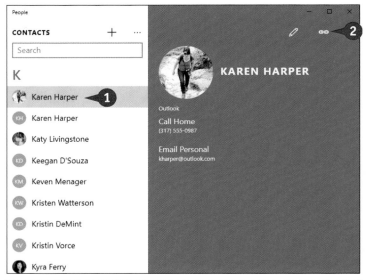

The Links for *Contact* screen appears (where *Contact* is the name of the contact you click in step **1**).

3 Click **Choose a contact to link**.

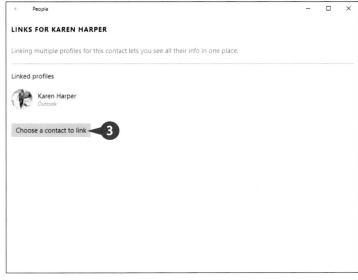

The Choose a Contact dialog box appears.

④ Click the contact you want to link.

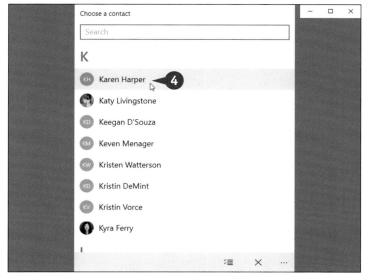

People links the contacts and returns you to the Links for *Contact* screen.

Ⓐ The linked contacts appear here.

⑤ Click **Back** (←) to return to the Contacts list.

The contact's Link icon (🔗) now displays the number of linked profiles.

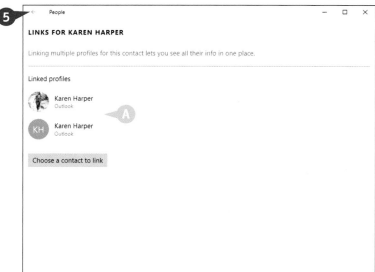

TIP

Can I remove a linked profile from a contact?

Yes. In some cases, you might find that you prefer to keep two separate profiles for a particular contact. For example, if you have separate business and personal profiles for a contact and both those profiles contain a great deal of information, you might find that the combined profile is too confusing or cluttered.

To unlink a profile from a contact, click the contact and then click **Link** (🔗). In the Links for *Contact* screen, click the linked profile that you want to remove. When People asks you to confirm, click **Unlink**.

View Your Calendar

Windows comes with a Calendar app to enable you to manage your schedule. To create an event such as an appointment or meeting, or an all-day event such as a conference or trip, you select the date when the event occurs.

Calendar lets you change the calendar view to suit your needs. For example, you can show just a single day's worth of events if you want to concentrate on that day's activities. Similarly, you can view a week's or a month's worth of events if you want to get a larger sense of what your overall schedule looks like.

View Your Calendar

View Events by Month

1 On the Start screen, click **Calendar** (not shown).

Note: When you first start Calendar, if Windows asks if the app can use your location, click **No**.

2 Click **Month**.

Your calendar for the month appears.

3 Move the mouse (�) and then click ∧ and ∨ to navigate the months.

Note: On a touchscreen PC, you navigate the months by swiping up and down on the screen.

View Events by Week

1 Click **Week**.

A To see just Monday through Friday, click **Work week** instead.

Your events for the week appear.

2 Move the mouse (�) and then click < and > to navigate the weeks.

Note: On a touchscreen PC, you navigate the weeks by swiping left and right on the screen.

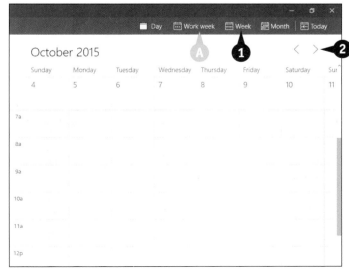

View Events by Day

1 Click **Day**.

The events for a single day appear.

2 Move the mouse (⮣) and then click **<** and **>** to navigate the days.

Note: On a touchscreen PC, you navigate the days by swiping left and right on the screen.

View Today's Events

1 Click **Today**.

Calendar navigates the current view to include today's date.

TIP

Are there any techniques that I can use to navigate the calendar?
Yes, you can use the mini calendar that appears on the left side of the Calendar window. If you do not see the mini calendar, click **Menu** (≡) in the upper left corner of the Calendar window. Position the mouse (⮣) over the mini calendar and then click ∧ and ∨ to navigate the months. (On a touchscreen PC, you navigate the months by swiping up and down on the mini calendar.) Then click the day you want to view.

Add an Event to Your Calendar

You can help organize your life by using the Calendar app to record your upcoming events — such as appointments, meetings, phone calls, and dates — on the date and time that they are scheduled to occur.

If the event has a set time and duration — for example, a meeting or a lunch date — you add the event directly to the calendar as a regular appointment. If the event has no set time — for example, a birthday, anniversary, or multiple-day event such as a sales meeting or vacation — you can create an all-day event.

Add an Event to Your Calendar

1 In the Calendar app, navigate to the date when the event occurs.

2 Click the time when the event starts.

Note: If you are currently in Month view, click the day the event occurs.

3 Type a name for the event.

4 Type the event location.

5 Click **More details**.

Calendar displays the event details screen.

6 If the start date and/or time is incorrect, use the Start controls to select the correct start time.

7 If the end date and/or time is incorrect, use the End controls to select the correct end time.

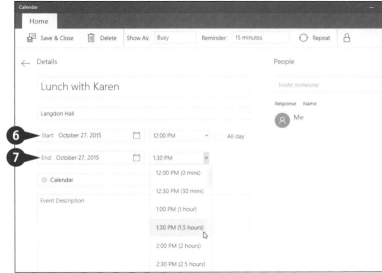

8 Use the large text area to type notes related to the event.

9 Click **Save & Close**.

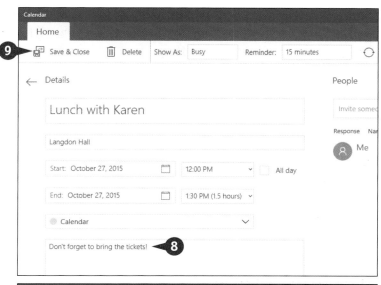

A Calendar adds the event to your schedule.

To make changes to the event, you can click it.

How do I set up an event that has no set time, such as an anniversary or conference?
Any activity that has no set time or that takes up one or more entire days is called an *all-day event*. Examples include birthdays, anniversaries, conferences, trade shows, and vacations. To specify such an event, follow steps **1** to **4** to start a new event, click **All day** (☐ changes to ☑), and then click **Done**. The all-day event appears as a banner at the top of the date when you are in Day or Week view.

Create a Recurring Event

If you have an activity or event that recurs at a regular interval, you can create an event and configure it to automatically repeat in the Calendar app. This saves you from having to repeatedly add the future events manually because Calendar adds them for you automatically.

You can repeat an event daily, weekly, monthly, or yearly. If your activity recurs every day only during the workweek, such as a staff meeting, you can also set up the event to repeat every weekday.

Create a Recurring Event

1 Follow the steps in the previous section, "Add an Event to Your Calendar," to create an event.

2 Click **Repeat**.

3 Click the repeat interval that you want to use.

A You might also be able to further refine your choice, such as choosing the specific day of the week for the Weekly interval.

4 If needed, use the End calendar control to select the last recurrence.

5 Click **Save & Close**.

Calendar adds the future events using the interval that you specified.

Note: To edit a recurring event, right-click it and then click either **Edit occurrence** to edit just that occurrence or **Edit series** to edit every occurrence.

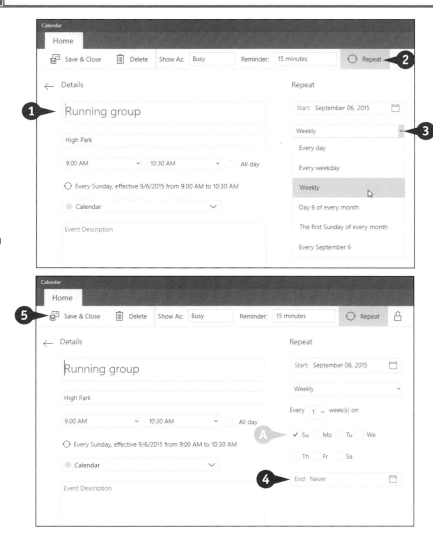

Add an Event Reminder

You can help make sure that you never miss a meeting, appointment, or other event by setting up the Calendar app to remind you before the event occurs. A *reminder* is a notification message that Windows displays at a specified time before the event occurs. By default, Calendar adds a 15-minute reminder to each event, but you can change that to a more suitable interval.

Add an Event Reminder

1 Follow the steps in the section "Add an Event to Your Calendar," earlier in this chapter, to create an event.

2 Click the **Reminder** ✔.

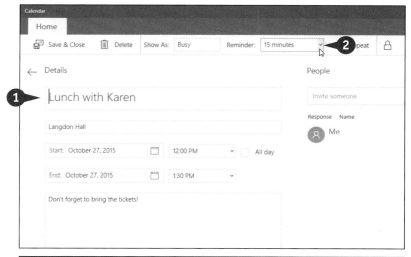

3 Click the length of time before the event that you want the reminder to appear.

4 Click **Save & Close**.

Calendar saves the event and later reminds you of it beforehand, according to the time that you select.

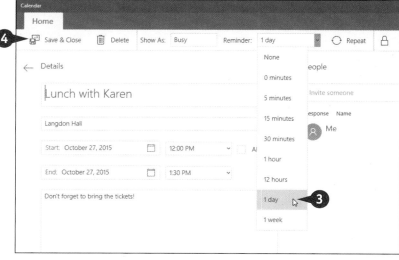

Send or Respond to an Event Invitation

The Calendar app has a feature that enables you to include people from your Contacts list in your event by sending them invitations to attend. If you receive an event invitation, you can respond to it to let the person organizing the event know whether you will be attending.

The advantage of this approach is that when other people respond to the invitation, Calendar automatically updates the event. When you receive an event invitation, the email message contains buttons that enable you to respond quickly.

Send or Respond to an Event Invitation

Send an Event Invitation

1 Follow the steps in the section "Add an Event to Your Calendar," earlier in this chapter, to create an event.

2 In the People list, specify a person that you want to invite:

If the person is in your Contacts list, type the person's name.

If the person is not in your Contacts, type the person's email address.

3 Press **Enter**.

4 Repeat steps **2** and **3** for each person you want to invite.

5 Type a note that will appear with the invitation.

6 Click **Send**.

Calendar saves the event and sends the invitation.

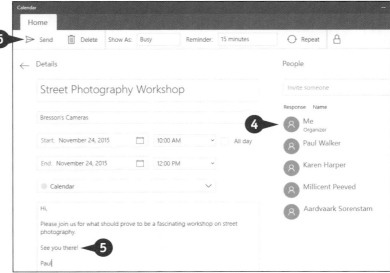

Handle an Event Invitation

1 Click **Mail** (✉).

Windows switches you to the Mail app.

2 Click the invitation.

3 Click the button that represents your reply:

Ⓐ Click **Accept** if you can attend the event.

Ⓑ Click **Tentative** if you are currently not sure whether you can attend.

Ⓒ Click **Decline** if you cannot attend the event.

4 If you clicked either Tentative or Decline, choose whether you want to edit your response, send the response right away, or not send a response.

5 Click **Calendar** (🖩) to return to the Calendar app.

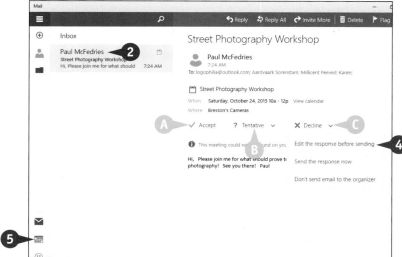

If I click Tentative, how do I later either accept or decline the invitation?

When you click **Tentative**, Windows temporarily adds the event to the Calendar at the date and time specified in the invitation. To respond definitively, open the event details and then click either **Accept** (✓) or **Decline** (✗).

If I am not sure whether to accept an invitation, can I check my calendar?

Yes. The invitation message includes a link to your calendar that automatically displays the date on which the event occurs. Click the message and then click **View calendar**. Windows opens the Calendar app and displays the event date so that you can check your schedule.

Customize Your Calendar

Calendar is a useful tool right out of the box, but it comes with a decent collection of customization settings that you can use to make the app even better. For example, you can specify a first day of the week other than Sunday. You can also specify which days are in your workweek and which hours are in your workday. You can also display week number and change the Calendar colors.

Customize Your Calendar

① Click **Settings** (⚙).

② Click **Calendar Settings**.

The Calendar Settings pane appears.

③ Click the **First Day of Week** ˅ and then click the day you prefer to use as the first of the week.

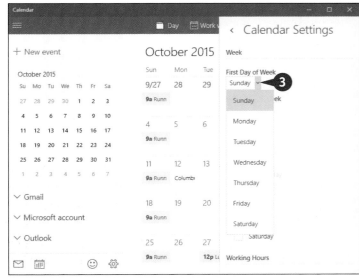

4 Use the **Days in Work Week** check boxes to define your workweek.

5 Click the **Start time** ⌄ and then click the **End time** ⌄ to define the beginning and end of your workday.

6 If you want to display week numbers in the calendar, click the **Week Numbers** ⌄ and then click an option (see the Tip for an explanation).

7 In the Calendar Color Options section, click the color option you prefer (○ changes to ●).

8 Click outside the Calendar Settings pane to close the pane.

Calendar puts the new settings into effect.

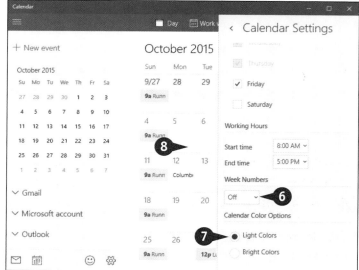

What is the difference between the two Week Number options?

Besides the default option of None, the Week Number list offers two numbering options:

First Day Of Year — If you select this option, Calendar designates week 1 as the week that contains January 1, even if that week contains one or more days from the previous year.

First Full Week — If you select this option, Calendar designates week 1 as the first full week that occurs in the year, even if the previous week contains one or more days from the current year.

Performing Day-to-Day Tasks with Apps

You can use the Windows apps to perform many useful tasks, including searching for apps, settings, and files; getting directions; looking up a weather forecast; tracking a stock; and getting the latest sports news.

Search Your PC

After you have used your PC for a while and have created many documents, you might have trouble locating a specific file. You can save a great deal of time by having Windows search for your document.

You can use the Search feature to look for apps, system settings, and documents on your PC, as well as websites on the Internet. If you are working with File Explorer, you can also perform document searches using the Search box in a folder window.

Search Your PC

Search from the Taskbar

1 Click inside the Search box and type your search text.

A Windows displays the top apps, settings, and documents with names that include your search text.

B Windows displays other search results here, organized by category (such as Settings).

C If you see the app, setting, or document that you want, you can click it.

2 If you do not see the item you want, click **My stuff**.

Windows displays a larger selection of search results.

3 Click the **Show** ∨ and then click a category.

Windows displays the category items that match your search text.

4 Click the item you want.

Windows opens the app, setting, document, or website.

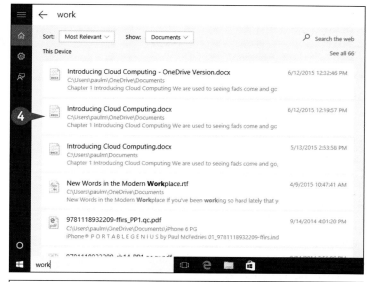

Search from a Folder Window

1 Click **File Explorer** (▢).

2 Open the folder you want to search.

3 Type your search text in the Search box.

D As you type, Windows displays the folders and documents in the current folder with names, contents, or keywords that match your search text.

4 If you see the folder or document that you want, double-click it.

The folder or document opens.

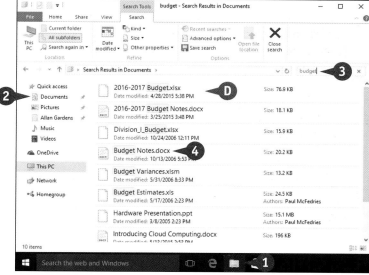

TIPS

Can I restrict my folder searches to a particular file type?
Yes, you can tell File Explorer to search only one of more than 20 different file types, including documents, music, and pictures. In File Explorer, click inside the Search box and then click the **Search** tab in the ribbon. Click the **Kind** ▼ and then click the type of file you want to find.

Is there any way to tell Windows that I specifically want to search for settings?
Not directly, but the Settings app does have a search feature. Click **Start** (▦), click **Settings**, and then use the Search box to type a word or phrase for the setting you want.

Configure the Cortana Voice Assistant

I f you have a microphone attached to your PC, you can use it to search for information on your computer and on the web by using voice commands. To set up this feature, you need to configure Cortana, the Windows 10 voice assistant. Cortana knows what is on your PC and what is available on the web. Although you can still type searches as described in the previous section, "Search Your PC," once Cortana is configured you can run searches and other tasks using verbal commands that you speak into your microphone.

Configure the Cortana Voice Assistant

1 Click inside the Search box.

Windows asks if you want to get started with Cortana.

2 Click **Next**.

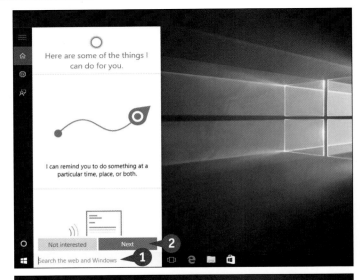

Windows displays the Cortana user agreement.

3 Click **I agree**.

Cortana asks you to enter your name.

④ Type your name (or whatever you would like Cortana to call you).

⑤ Click **Next**.

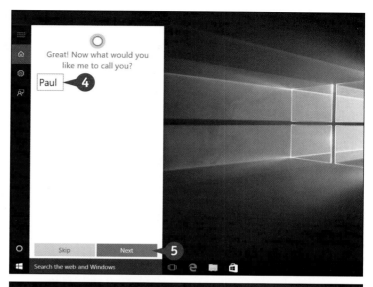

Cortana displays some sample interests.

⑥ Click **Got it**.

You can now use Cortana to search your PC.

How do I use Cortana?
Display the taskbar and then click **Talk** (🎤) inside the Search box. You then see the prompt "Ask me anything" in the Search box. You can then either speak your search text or specify an action, such as calling a contact, creating a calendar entry, setting an alarm or reminder, or taking a note.

How do I adjust Cortana's settings?
Click inside the Search box, click **Menu** (≡), and then click **Settings**. To change the name Cortana uses for you, click **Change my name**. If you no longer want to use Cortana, click the **Cortana** switch to **Off**.

Display a Location on a Map

You can use the Maps app to display a location on a map. *Maps* is a Metro app that displays digital maps that you can use to view just about any location by searching for an address or place name.

When you first start the Maps app, Windows asks if it can turn on location services, which are background features that help determine your current location and offer this information to apps such as Maps. For the best results with Maps, you should allow Windows to turn on location services.

Display a Location on a Map

1 In the taskbar's Search box, type **maps**.

2 Click **Maps**.

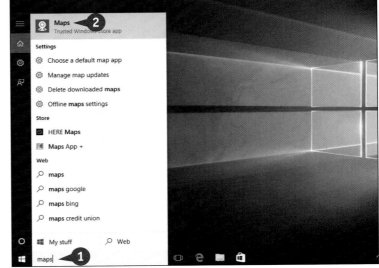

The first time that you start Maps, the app asks if it can use your location.

3 Click **Yes**.

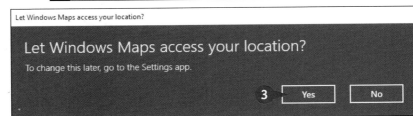

4 Type the address or the name of the location.

5 Click the location in the search results.

A To see a list of matching locations, you can click **Search** (🔍) and then click the location you want.

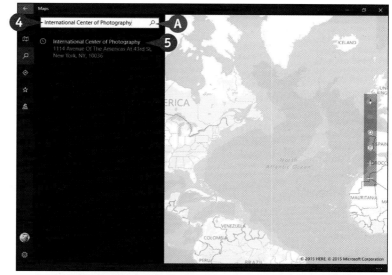

B Maps displays the location on the map.

C Maps displays information about the location.

D You can click **Zoom in** (⊞) and **Zoom out** (⊟) to see more or less map detail.

E You can click **Show my location** (◎) to see your current location.

F You can click **Back** (←) to hide the location information.

TIPS

How does Maps know my location?
First, it looks for known *Wi-Fi hotspots*, which are commercial establishments that offer wireless Internet access. Second, if you are connected to the Internet, Maps uses the location information embedded in your unique Internet Protocol (IP) address. Third, if your PC has a Global Positioning System (GPS) receiver, Maps uses this GPS data to pinpoint your location to within a few feet.

Can I turn off location services?
Yes. Click **Start** (⊞) and then click **Settings**. In the Settings app, click **Privacy**, click **Location**, and then click the **Location** switch to **Off**.

Get Directions to a Location

Besides displaying locations, Maps also recognizes the roads and highways found in most cities, states, and countries. This means that you can use the Maps app to get specific directions for traveling from one location to another.

You specify a starting point and destination for a trip, and Maps then provides you with directions for getting from one point to the other. Maps highlights the trip route on a digital map and also gives you specific details for negotiating each leg of the trip.

Get Directions to a Location

1 Click **Directions** ().

2 Click the travel method: **Driving** (), **Transit** (), or **Walking** ().

Note: Maps assumes that you want to start at your current location. If that is true, skip step **3**.

3 Type the name or address of the location where your journey will begin.

4 Type the name or address of your destination and then press Enter.

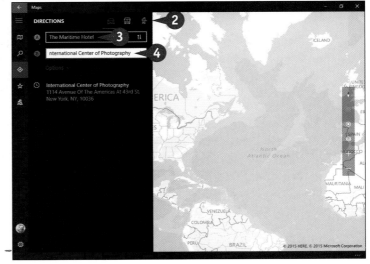

Ⓐ Maps displays an overview of the route.

Ⓑ This area tells the distance and approximate traveling time by the chosen travel method.

Ⓒ This area displays the various legs of the journey.

❺ Click the first leg of the trip.

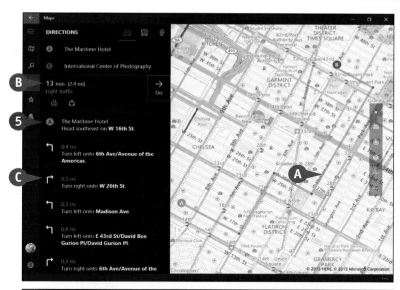

Maps zooms in to show you just that leg of the trip.

❻ As you complete each leg of the trip, click the next leg for further instructions.

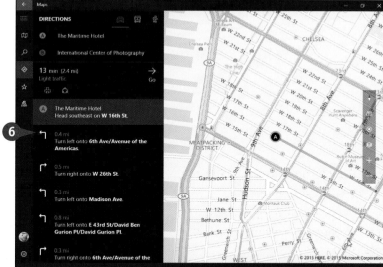

TIP

Can I get traffic information as I follow the directions provided by Maps?
Yes. Click **Map views** (⬚) and then click **Traffic** to see the current traffic conditions:

- Green means traffic is moving normally on that route.
- Yellow means traffic is slower than normal.
- Orange tells you that traffic is slow.
- Red means traffic is heavy.

Check Your Weather Forecast

You can use the Weather app to view your city's current conditions and five-day forecast. The Weather app takes advantage of the MSN Weather service provided by Microsoft, which uses several online weather resources to obtain up-to-the-minute conditions and forecasts.

The Weather app can check the forecast for a default location that your specify, or for your current location, which uses Windows location services to determine your location and display the forecast. If you would prefer to see the forecast for some other location, see the next section, "Check Another City's Weather Forecast."

Check Your Weather Forecast

Create a Default Location Forecast

1 Click **Start** (⊞).

2 Click **Weather**.

The Weather app appears. The first time you start the program, it asks you to specify a default temperature unit and location.

3 Click **Fahrenheit** or **Celsius** (○ changes to ⊙).

4 Begin typing the name of the default location you want to use.

5 When you see the location in the list, click it.

Weather displays the location's current conditions and forecast.

Check Your Current Location Forecast

1 Click **Settings** (⚙).

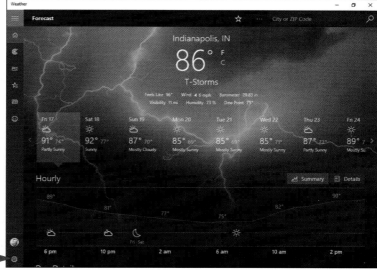

2 Click **Always detect my location** (○ changes to ⦿).

Weather determines your current location.

3 Click **Back** (←).

Weather displays your current location's conditions and forecast.

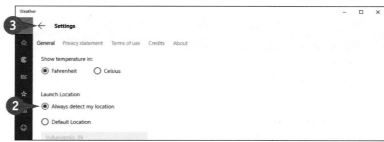

TIPS

Why does the Weather app say, "Your location cannot be found"?
You have turned off location services. Click **Start** (⊞), click **Settings**, click **Privacy**, click **Location**, and then click the **Location** switch to **On**. Click the **MSN Weather** switch to **On**.

How can I see my city's forecast when I start the Weather app?
If your city is the only one added to Weather, then you see your forecast when you start the app. Otherwise, make your city the app's default location. To do this, open the Weather app, click **Settings** (⚙), click **Default Location** (○ changes to ⦿), and then type the name of your city in the text box.

Check Another City's Weather Forecast

You can use the Weather app to view another city's current conditions and five-day forecast. The Bing Weather service uses online resources to obtain up-to-the-minute information on the current conditions and weather forecasts for hundreds of locations around the world. If you are going to be traveling to another city or if you are simply curious about the weather conditions elsewhere, you can use Maps to look up the weather forecast for most cities around the world.

Check Another City's Weather Forecast

1 In the Weather app, click **Menu** (≡).

The menu appears.

2 Click **Places**.

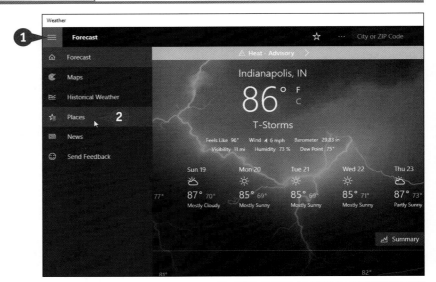

The Places screen appears.

3 Click **Add** (+).

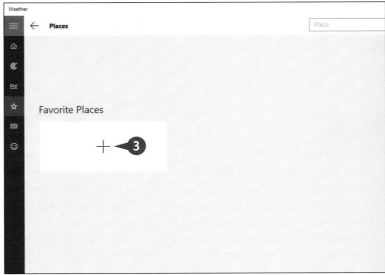

④ Type the name of the city whose weather you want to view.

Ⓐ As you type, Weather displays place names that match.

⑤ When you see the location that you want, click it.

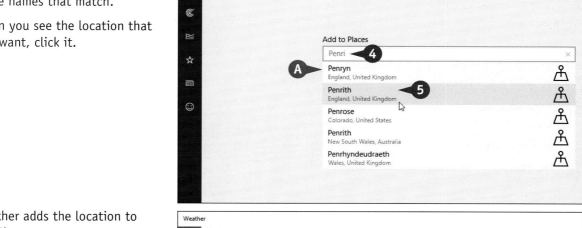

Ⓑ Weather adds the location to the Places screen.

⑥ Click the location.

Weather displays the city's current conditions and forecast.

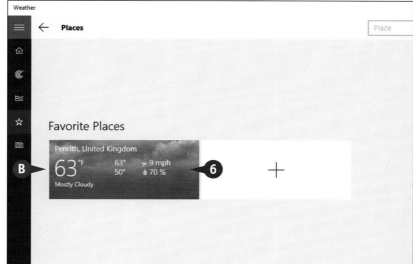

TIPS

How do I switch between Fahrenheit and Celsius?
In the Weather app, click **Menu** (≡) and then click **Settings** to open the Weather app's Settings pane with the General tab displayed. Then click either **Fahrenheit** or **Celsius** (○ changes to ◉).

How do I remove a city?
To remove a location from the Places screen, follow steps **1** and **2** to display the Places screen, right-click the city that you want to remove, and then click **Remove from Favorites** (✕).

Perform Calculations

You can use the Calculator app to make calculations and to convert numbers from one unit to another. The app comes with a Standard calculator that you can use or basic calculations such as addition, subtraction, multiplication, and division. For more advanced calculation, use either the Scientific or the Programmer calculator.

Calculator also comes with a number of converters that you can use to one value to a different unit. For example, you can use the Length converter to change centimeters to inches, or the Weight and Mass converter to change kilograms to pounds.

Perform Calculations

Start the Calculator
1. In the Search box, type **calc**.
2. Click **Calculator**.

The Calculator app appears.

Select a Calculator or Converter
1. Click **Menu** (☰).
2. Click the calculator or converter you want to use.

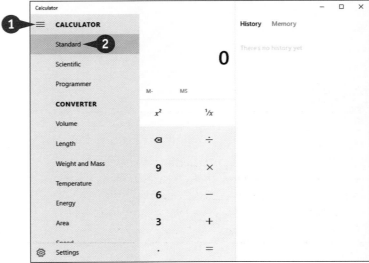

Perform a Calculation

1 Click the numeric buttons to enter a number.

2 Click an operator.

3 Repeat steps **1** and **2** as needed.

4 Click **Equals** =.

Calculator displays the result.

Perform a Conversion

1 Click the top ⌄ and then click the unit you want to convert from.

2 Click the bottom ⌄ and then click the unit you want to convert to.

3 Click the numeric buttons to enter the value you want to convert.

A Calculator displays the converted value.

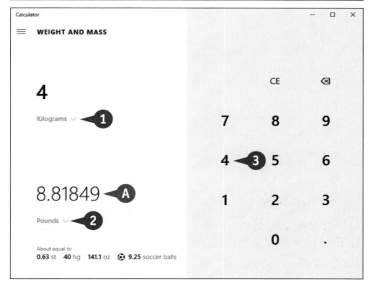

TIPS

What is the Calculator app's Memory feature and how do I use it?

The Memory feature lets you perform a calculation, save the result, then use that result as part of another calculation. To save a result to memory, perform the calculation and then click the **M+** button. To retrieve the result from memory, click the **MR** button.

Is there a way to rerun an earlier calculation?

Yes. Calculator saves your last few calculations in the History tab. To rerun a calculation, click **History** and then click the calculation. Note that you might need to scroll down the History list to see the calculation you want.

Get the Latest News

You can use the News app to read the latest news stories and to locate stories that are important to you. The News app aggregates news stories from a wide variety of web sources, including the Associated Press, Reuters, *The New York Times*, and CNN.

The News app's main page — called *Headlines* — displays stories in various categories, including Technology, Business, Politics, and Sports. If you are interested in other topics, you can customize News to show stories related to those topics.

Get the Latest News

1 Click **Start** (⊞).

2 Click **News**.

The News app appears.

3 Click a category.

You can also scroll up and down to see the main stories in each category.

4 Click **Menu** (≡).

5 Click **Interests**.

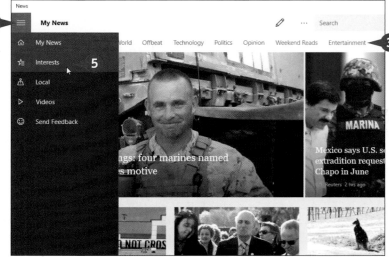

The Interests page appears.

6 To add a new section, click **Add an Interest** (+).

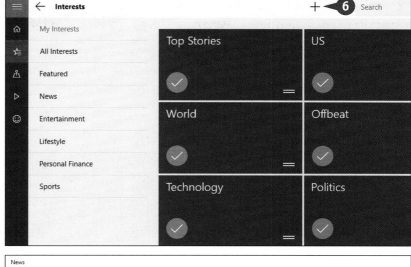

The Add an Interest screen appears.

7 Type the name of the topic that you want to add.

Ⓐ News displays topics that match.

8 Click the topic that you want to add.

News adds the topic to the Topics page.

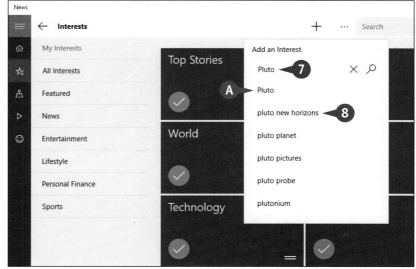

TIPS

Can I see news that focuses on a particular country?

Yes. To see news from a particular country, click **Menu** (≡), and then click **Settings** to open the News app's Settings pane with the General tab displayed. Use the **Choose edition** list to select the country whose news you want to view.

Can I see news that focuses on my current location?

Yes. To see news related to your location, click **Menu** (≡) and then click **Local**. When the app asks if it can use your location, click **Yes**. News displays stories and sources that are associated with your PC's current location.

Track a Stock

You can use the Money app to read the latest financial news stories, see the latest financial data, and create a list of stocks to track. The Finance app combines a wide variety of financial information in a single place.

The Money app's main screen — called *Home* — displays financial news; Dow statistics, NASDAQ information, and other index values; major stock activity; bond prices; interest rates; and more. You can also use the Money app to create a list — called a *watchlist* — of the stocks that you want to track.

Track a Stock

1 Click **Start** (⊞).

2 Click **Money**.

The Money app appears.

A To read the latest financial information, click a category.

You can also scroll up, left, and down to see the latest financial news and data.

3 Click **Menu** (≡).

4 Click **Watchlist**.

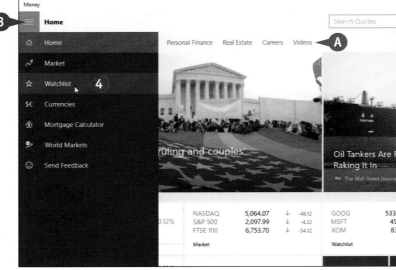

The Watchlist screen appears.

5 Click **Add** (+).

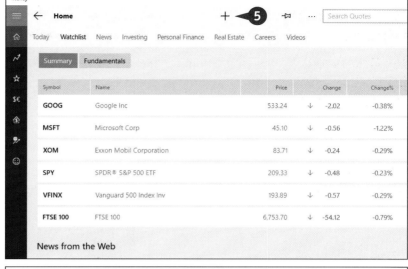

The Add to Watchlist screen appears.

6 Type the stock symbol or name of the stock that you want to add.

B As you type, Money displays stocks that match.

7 When you see the stock that you want, click it.

Money adds the stock to the Watchlist screen.

Note: Your watchlist also appears on the MSN Finance screen.

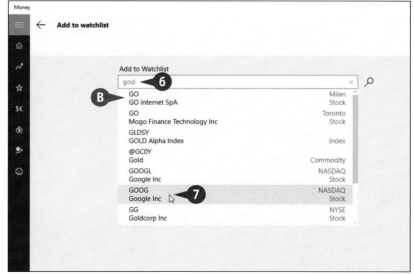

TIPS

How do I remove a stock from my watchlist?

Follow steps **1** to **4** to display the Watchlist screen, click **Edit** (✎), and then click **Remove** (✕) beside each stock you no longer want on the watchlist.

Is there a way to keep my watchlist on-screen so that I can monitor it?

Yes, you can snap Money to the edge of the screen. In Money, display the Watchlist screen. Now press ⊞+← to snap the window to the left side of the screen. If you prefer to snap the Money window to the right side, press and hold ⊞ and tap → until the window is in the position you want.

Follow Your Favorite Teams

You can use the Sports app to catch up on all your sports news. The Sports app combines a wide variety of sports news and information in a single place.

The Sports app's main screen — called *MSN Sports* — displays the top story of the day, other sports news, the day's schedule of upcoming games, and the latest scores from those games. You can also use the Sports app to create a list — called *My Favorites* — of the teams that you want to follow.

Follow Your Favorite Teams

1 Click **Start** (⊞).

2 Click **Sports**.

The Sports app appears.

Ⓐ To read the latest sports information, click a category.

You can also scroll up, left, and down to see the latest sports news, schedules, and scores.

3 Click **Menu** (≡).

The menu appears.

4 Click **My Favorites**.

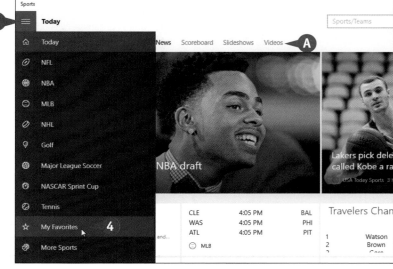

The My Favorites screen appears.

5 Click **Add** (+).

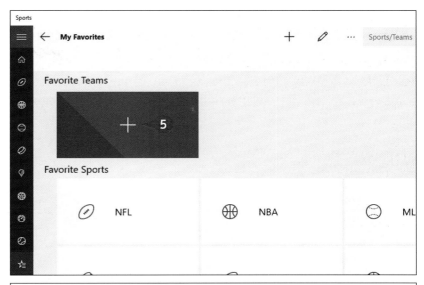

The Add to Favorites screen appears.

6 Type the name of the team that you want to add.

B As you type, Sports displays teams that match.

7 When you see the team that you want, click it.

Sports adds the team to the My Favorites page.

8 Repeat steps **5** to **7** for every team that you want to follow.

You can now see news, schedules, and stats by clicking a team in the My Favorites list.

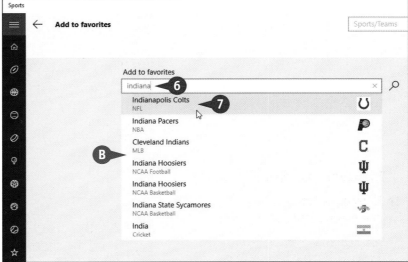

TIPS

How do I remove a team from my Favorite Teams list?
Follow steps **1** to **4** to display the My Favorites section. Click **Edit** (✏) and then click **Remove** (✗) beside each team you no longer want to follow.

Can I see more information about a particular sport?
Yes, the Sports app offers information on several sports leagues, including the National Football League, the National Basketball Association, Major League Baseball, and the National Hockey League. For each league, you see the latest news stories, a schedule of upcoming games, recent results, current standings, player statistics, and more. To select a league, click **Menu** (≡) and then click a league in the menu.

Find a Recipe

The Food & Drink app enables you to look up a recipe based on one or more filters such as cooking method, cuisine, major ingredients, and dietary restrictions. You can also add your own recipes to the app.

The Food & Drink app gets information from the MSN Food & Drink site, so you can also use the app to get the latest news on food and nutrition, learn about cooking tools and techniques, and read about famous chefs. You can also get information on wine and cocktails.

Find a Recipe

1 In the Search box, type **food**.

2 Click **Food & Drink**.

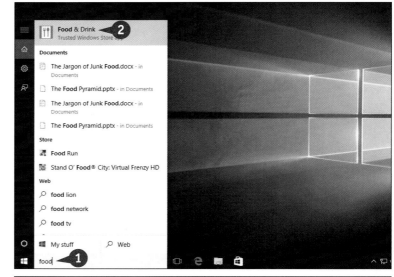

The Food & Drink app appears.

3 Right-click the screen.

The application bar appears.

Ⓐ To read the latest food- and drink-related news and information, click a category.

You can also scroll left and right to see the latest news.

4 Click **Recipes**.

The Browse Recipes screen appears.

5 Click a filter type.

6 Click a specific filter.

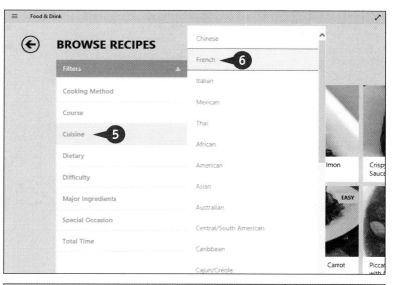

B Food & Drink adds the filter.

7 Repeat steps **5** and **6** to add other filters to your search.

8 When you see a recipe you want to view, click it.

Food & Drink opens the recipe.

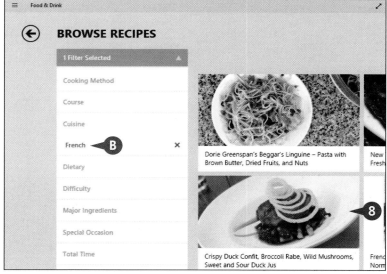

TIPS

Can I save a recipe?
Yes, you can create a *collection* and add the recipe to that list. Follow steps **2** to **8** to view the recipe. Click **Add to Collections**, click **Create a new collection**, type a name, and then click **Add**. To view your collections, right-click the screen, scroll the app bar to the right, and then click **Collections**.

How do I add my own recipes to the Food & Drink app?
Scroll right from the MSN Food & Drink home page and then click **Add a Recipe**. In the Add a Recipe page, use the tabs on the left — Overview, Photos, Ingredients, Steps, and Notes — to enter the recipe, and then click **Save**.

Look Up Health Information

You can use the Health & Fitness app to read the latest news stories related to fitness, nutrition, medicine, and medical symptoms.

The app's main page — called *MSN Health & Fitness* — displays the latest health news as well as information organized into various categories, including Exercises, Workouts, Nutrition, and Symptom Checker. You can also use Health & Fitness to track your diet and workouts.

Look Up Health Information

1 In the Search box, type **health**.

2 Click **Health & Fitness**.

The Health & Fitness app appears.

3 From the MSN Health & Fitness home page, scroll left and right to see the main stories in each category.

4 Right-click the screen.

A The application bar appears.

5 Click **Exercises** to look up specific exercises.

6 Click **Workouts** to locate workouts based on type, body part, and more.

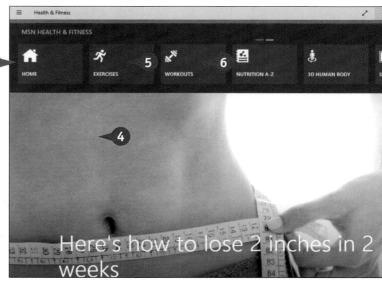

7 Click **Nutrition A-Z** to look up information in the nutrition encyclopedia.

8 Click **3D Human Body** to learn about the human body using 3D images.

9 Click **Symptom Checker** to look up symptoms.

10 Scroll right.

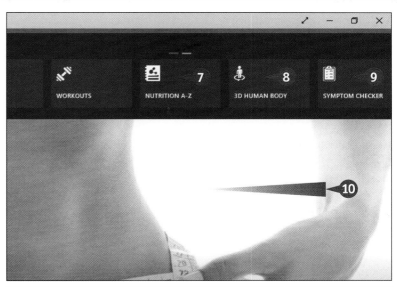

11 Use the trackers to track your exercise and diet (see the Tips).

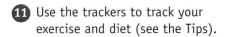

TIPS

How do I log the calories I eat?
Use the Diet Tracker to enter what you eat. The Diet Tracker calculates the calories and shows your daily total. From the app home page, scroll right and click **Diet Tracker**. Edit the Target calories value. Click **+ Food**, search for the food you want to add, select it, specify the amount, and then click **Done**.

How do I keep a log of my workouts?
Use the Cardio Tracker to enter your workouts. From the app home page, scroll right and click **Cardio Tracker**. Click **+ Exercise**, search for the workout type (such as Running), select it, enter the duration and/or distance, and then click **Done**.

Set an Alarm

You can use the Alarms & Clock app to set an alarm to play at a specific time. You can set up the alarm to play once or you can have it repeat on specified days. You can also choose the sound that Windows plays when the alarm goes off. Note that your PC must be turned on and awake for the alarm feature to work.

You can also use the Alarms & Clock app to set up a timer that counts down from a specified number of hours, minutes, and seconds, and to run a stopwatch for timing an event.

Set an Alarm

1 In the Search box, type **alarms**.

2 Click **Alarms & Clock**.

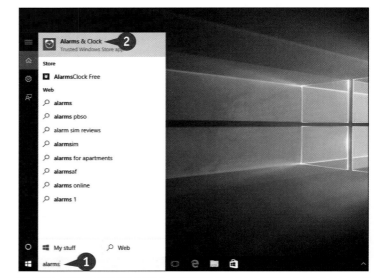

The Alarms app appears.

A Alarms comes with a default alarm already added. To modify this alarm, click it and then follow steps **4** to **10**.

B Click **On/Off** to toggle the alarm on or off.

3 Click **New** (+).

④ Type a name for the alarm.

⑤ Set the time of the alarm.

⑥ Click **Repeats** and then click
the check box beside each day
you want the alarm to ring
(☐ changes to ☑).

⑦ Click **Sound** and then click a
sound to play.

⑧ Click **Snooze time** and then
click the interval the app uses
when you select Snooze.

⑨ Click **Save** (💾).

Ⓒ Alarms adds and activates the
alarm.

Ⓓ To delete an alarm, click
Manage (☷), and then click
Delete (🗑) beside the alarm.

TIPS

How do I set a timer?
At the top of the Alarms & Clock app, click **Timer** and then click the
displayed time to open the Edit Timer window. Edit the timer name and then
use the Duration boxes to set the number of hours, minutes, and seconds
for the timer. Click **Save** (💾). When you are ready to start the timer,
click **Play** (▷).

How do I use the stopwatch?
At the top of the Alarms &
Clock app, click **Stopwatch**.
Click **Play** (▷) to start the
watch. To get a lap or split
time, click **Laps/Splits** (🏳).

Write a Note

You can use the Notepad app to create simple text documents for things such as to-do lists and meeting notes. Word processing programs such as WordPad, as well as powerful note-taking apps such as the OneNote app covered in Chapter 9, are useful for creating complex and lengthy documents, but they feel like overkill when all you want to do is jot down a few simple notes. For these more basic text tasks, the Notepad app that comes with Windows is perfect because it offers a simple interface that is easy to learn and use.

Write a Note

Start Notepad

1 Click **Start** (▦).

The Start menu appears.

2 Click **All apps**.

A All Apps changes to Back.

3 Click **Windows Accessories**.

4 Click **Notepad**.

Notepad opens.

Write and Save a Note

1 Type your note text.

2 Click **File**.

3 Click **Save**.

The Save As dialog box appears.

4 Type a name for the file.

5 Click **Save**.

Notepad saves the file.

TIPS

Can I create a temporary note?
Yes. If you just want to jot down a phone number, you can create the Windows equivalent of a sticky note by following steps 1 to 4 in the subsection "Start Notepad" and then clicking **Sticky Notes**.

What is the difference between Notepad and WordPad?
Notepad is called a *text editor* and you use it only to enter and edit text. WordPad is called a *word processing program* and you use it not only to enter and edit text, but also to format that text with fonts, sizes, and colors; apply bulleted and numbered lists; insert images; and more.

Working with Images

Whether you load your images from a digital camera or a scanner, download them from the Internet, or draw them yourself, Windows comes with a number of useful tools for working with those images. In this chapter, you learn how to import images from a camera, view your images, fix photo problems, and delete images.

Import Images from a Digital Camera

You can import photos from a digital camera and save them on your PC. If your camera stores the photos on a memory card, you can also use a memory card reader attached to your PC to upload the digital photos from the removable drive that Windows sets up when you insert the card.

To perform the import directly from your digital camera, you need a cable to connect your camera to your PC. Most digital cameras come with a USB cable. After you have the digital photos on your system, you can view or print the images.

Import Images from a Digital Camera

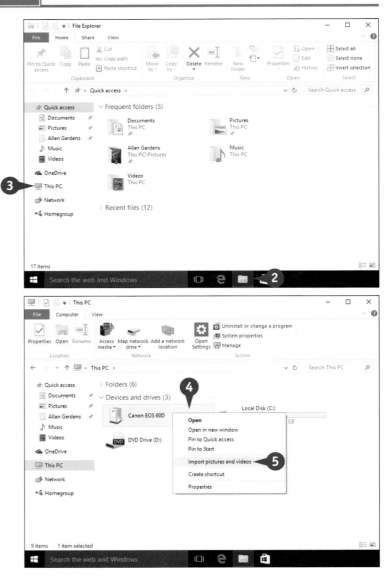

1 Plug in your camera or memory storage card reader.

Note: If you see a notification, click the notification and then skip to step **5**.

2 Click **File Explorer** (📁).

3 Click **This PC**.

File Explorer displays a list of the devices attached to your PC.

4 Right-click your digital camera.

5 Click **Import pictures and videos**.

The Import Pictures and Videos dialog box appears.

6 Click **Import all new items now** (○ changes to ●).

7 Type a name to use for the import.

8 Click **Import**.

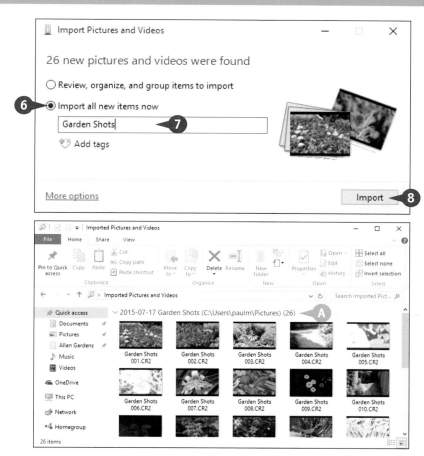

Windows imports the photos.

When the import is complete, File Explorer displays your imported photos.

A The Photos app stores the imported photos in your Pictures library in a folder named after today's date.

How can I import just some of the photos on my camera?
If you want to import only a subset of your photos, follow steps **1** to **5** to open the Import Pictures and Videos dialog box. Click **Review, organize, and groups items to import** (□ changes to ☑) and then click **Next**. You now see the camera photos grouped by date. Click **Select all** (● changes to ○) to deselect all the groups. Click the check box (□ changes to ☑) and type a name for each group you want to import, and then click **Import**.

Scan an Image

You can create a digital copy of a photo or other image by using a document scanner, or the scanner component of an all-in-one printer. The scanner copies the image to your computer, where you can then store it as a file on your hard drive.

You can use a scanned image in many ways. For example, you can scan a photo to email to friends or publish on a web page. You can also scan a logo or other image to use in a document.

Scan an Image

1 Turn on your scanner or all-in-one printer and position a photo or other image on the scanner bed.

2 In the Search box, type **scan**.

3 Click **Scan**.

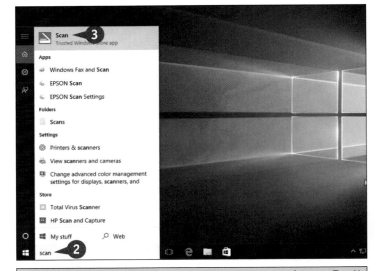

The Scan window appears.

4 Use the File Type list to select the file type you want to use for the scanned image file.

5 Click **Show more**.

The Scan window displays extra settings.

6 Use the Color Mode list to select a mode that matches your image: Color, Grayscale, or Black and White.

7 Use the Resolution list to specify the scan resolution.

Note: The higher the resolution, the sharper the image, but the larger the resulting file.

8 Click **Preview**.

A A preview of the scan appears here.

9 Click and drag the corners of the rectangle to set the scan area.

10 Click **Scan**.

Windows scans the image.

TIPS

How do I view a picture I have previously scanned?
Windows stores the image in the Scans folder in the Pictures library. To select a different location, follow steps **1** to **5**, click the **Scans** link under Save File To, and then select a new folder.

What other methods can I use to scan an image?
Scanners and all-in-one printers come with a Scan button that you can push to start a new scan. You can also use the Search box to type **fax**, click **Windows Fax and Scan**, and then click **New Scan**. In Paint (type **paint** and then click **Paint**), click **File** and then click **From scanner or camera**.

Navigate the Pictures Library

Before you can work with your images, you need to view them on your PC. You do that by using the Photos app to open the Pictures library, which is a special folder designed specifically for storing images.

To get more out of the Pictures library, you need to know not only how to open it, but also the basic techniques for opening any albums that you have stored in the library.

Navigate the Pictures Library

① Click **File Explorer** (▭).

The File Explorer program window appears.

② Click **Pictures**.

The Pictures library appears.

Ⓐ Items with folder icons are subfolders.

Ⓑ Items without folder icons are individual images.

③ Double-click a subfolder.

File Explorer displays the subfolder's images.

Do I have to use File Explorer to navigate the Pictures library?
No. Although File Explorer is often the easiest and fastest way to navigate the Picture library, it is not the only way. An alternative method is to use the Photos app, which you launch by clicking **Start** (⊞) and then clicking **Photos**. You can then use the icons on the left to view the pictures by collection (▦) or by album (▦). See the next section, "View Your Images," for more information.

View Your Images

If you want to look at several images, Windows gives you two methods to navigate backward and forward through the images in the Pictures library. First, you can use File Explorer to open an individual image for viewing in the Photos app, and then navigate through the other images in the same folder. Second, you can use the Photos app directly to view your images by collection or by album.

View Your Images

View Individual Images

1 In File Explorer, open the folder that contains the images you want to view.

Note: See the previous section, "Navigate the Pictures Library," for details.

2 Double-click the first image that you want to view.

The image appears in the Photos app.

3 Click the right-pointing arrow (>) to scroll right.

The Photos app displays the next screen of images from the album.

4 Repeat step 3 to continue viewing the album images.

Ⓐ You can return to the previous screen of images by scrolling left.

You can also press ➡ to see the next image and ⬅ to see the previous image.

View Images by Collection or Album

1 Click **Start** (⊞).

2 Click **Photos**.

The Photos app appears.

3 Click **Collection** (▦).

Ⓑ Alternatively, click **Albums** (▦) to view your pictures by album.

4 Scroll up and down to view your images by collection or album.

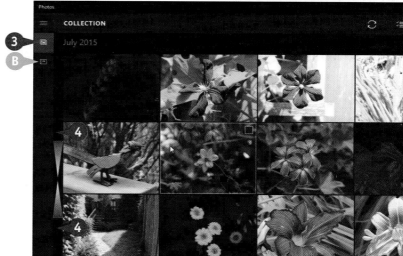

Can I view an individual picture in a collection or album?

Yes. Scroll to the image you want to view and then click it. You can then navigate the images as described in the subsection "View Individual Images." To return to the collection or album, click the screen to display the controls, and then click the name of the collection or album that appears in the upper left corner of the screen.

Start a Slide Show

Instead of viewing your photos one at a time, you can easily view multiple photos by running them in a slide show. You can run the slide show from within the Photos app. The slide show displays each photo for a few seconds and then automatically moves on to the next photo.

Alternatively, you can view a slide show of images using the Photos tile on the Start menu. This slide show uses recent images from your Pictures library.

Start a Slide Show

In the Photos App

1 In the Photos app, display the collection or album that contains the photos you want to display in your slide show.

2 Click the first image you want to display in the slide show.

Photos opens the image.

3 If you do not see the application bar, click the screen.

The Photos application bar appears.

4 Click **Slide show** (▣).

The Photos app begins the slide show.

On the Photos Tile

1 In the Photos app, click **Settings** (⚙).

The Settings window appears.

2 In the Choose What to Show on the Photos Tile list, select **Recent photos**.

The next time that you display the Start screen, the Photos tile displays a slide show of recent images from your Pictures library.

TIP

Can I change the speed at which the slide show displays the images?
No, not with the Photos app. However, you can adjust the speed if you start the slide show from File Explorer. Click **File Explorer** (▭) on the taskbar, open the **Pictures** library, and then click the folder that you want to view. In the ribbon, click the **Manage** tab and then click **Slide show** to start the show. To control the speed, right-click the screen to display the shortcut menu, and then click the speed that you want: **Slow**, **Medium**, or **Fast**.

Repair an Image

You can use Photos to improve the look of digital photos and other images. When you open an image in Photos, the application bar offers a number of tools for repairing various image attributes.

The easiest way to repair an image is to use the Auto Fix tool, which automatically adjusts an image's brightness, contrast, color temperature, tint, and saturation. You can also correct any of these elements manually, as well as remove red eye and hide photo flaws.

Repair an Image

Repair an Image Automatically

1 In Photos, display the image you want to repair.

2 If you do not see the application bar, click the screen.

Photos displays the application bar.

3 Click **Auto fix** ().

Photos repairs the image automatically.

Repair an Image Manually

1 In Photos, display the image you want to repair.

2 If you do not see the application bar, click the screen.

Photos displays the application bar.

3 Click **Edit** (✏).

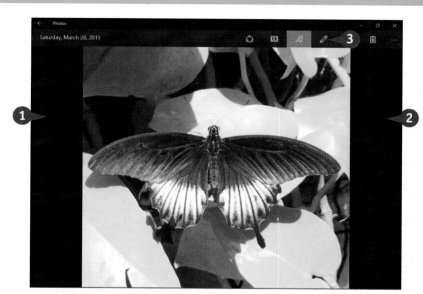

Photos displays the image editing tools.

4 Use the tools to repair the image as needed.

5 Click **Save** (🖫).

Photos saves your changes.

A If you prefer to leave the original as is, click **Save a Copy** (🖫) instead.

How do I remove red eye from a photo?
When you take a picture with a flash, the light may reflect off the subjects' retinas, resulting in red eye. To fix this, follow steps **1** to **3** in the subsection "Repair an Image Manually," click **Basic fixes**, click **Red eye**, and then click each red eye.

Can I remove a small flaw in a photo?
Yes. Photos offers a Retouch tool that enables you to perform a *spot fix*, which replaces an element from the photo with colors from the surrounding area. To perform a spot fix, follow steps **1** to **3** in the subsection "Repair an Image Manually," click **Basic fixes**, click **Retouch**, and then click the flaw.

Add a Photo Effect

You can use Photos to enhance the look of an image by applying one or more of the effects offered by the Photos app.

The Vignette effect darkens the edges and corners of the photo, which adds a natural frame around the image and draws attention to the rest of the photo. The Selective Focus effect enables you to select a custom circular or elliptical area of the photo that remains in focus while the area outside the selection gets blurred. This enables you to really attract the viewer's eye to a particular part of the photo.

Add a Photo Effect

Display the Effects

1 In Photos, display the image you want to repair.

2 If you do not see the application bar, click the screen.

The application bar appears.

3 Click **Edit** (✏️).

Photos displays the image editing tools.

4 Click **Effects**.

5 Click the effect you want to apply:

Ⓐ You can click **Vignette** to apply the Vignette effect. In this case, proceed with the subsection "Apply a Vignette Effect."

Ⓑ You can click **Selective focus** to apply the Selective Focus effect. In this case, proceed with the subsection "Apply a Selective Focus Effect."

Apply a Vignette Effect

1 Click and drag the vignette indicator clockwise until the vignette is at the level you want.

Note: If you apply too much vignette, drag the indicator counterclockwise to reduce the effect.

Apply a Selective Focus Effect

1 Move the mouse (↖) inside the selective focus area (↖ changes to ✥).

2 Drag the selective focus area to the portion of the photo that you want to remain in focus.

3 Click **Apply** (✔).

4 Click **Save** (🖫) (not shown).

Photos saves your changes.

TIPS

How do I change the shape of the selective focus area?

By default, the selective focus area is a circle. This works best for most photos, but if you have a non-circular area, you can adjust the shape of the selective focus area by dragging any of the four white circles that appear on the border of the selective focus area.

Can I control the amount of blur in the Selective Focus effect?

Yes. Photos offers several blur strengths that you can apply. Follow steps **1** to **3** to display the Selective Focus tool. Click **Strength** (🌀) and then click the blur level you prefer: Maximum, Strong, Medium (the default), Weak, or Minimum.

Crop an Image

If you have an image containing elements that you do not want or need to see, you can often cut out those elements. This is called *cropping*, and you can do this with Photos. When you crop a photo, you specify a rectangular area of the photo that you want to keep. Photos discards everything outside the rectangle.

Cropping is a useful skill to have because it can help give focus to the true subject of a photo. Cropping is also useful for removing extraneous elements that appear on or near the edges of a photo.

Crop an Image

1 In Photos, display the image you want to crop.

2 If you do not see the application bar, click the screen.

The application bar appears.

3 Click **Edit** (✐).

Photos displays the image editing tools.

4 Click **Basic fixes**.

5 Click **Crop**.

Photos displays a cropping rectangle on the photo.

6 Click and drag the photo or any corner of the rectangle to define the area you want to keep.

Note: Remember that Photos keeps the area inside the rectangle.

7 Click **Apply** (✓).

Photos applies the cropping.

8 Click **Save** (🖫).

Photos saves your changes.

Ⓐ If you prefer to leave the original as is, click **Save a copy** (🖫) instead.

TIP

Is there a quick way to crop a photo to a certain size?
Yes. Photos enables you to choose a specific ratio, such as 4 × 6 or 5 × 7. Repeat steps **1** to **5** to display the cropping rectangle over the image. Click **Aspect ratio** (▣). Click the ratio you want to use, such as 4 × 6 or 5 × 7. Repeat steps **7** and **8** to apply and save the cropping.

Rotate an Image

You can rotate and straighten an image using Photos. Depending on how you hold your camera when you take a shot, the resulting photo might show the subject sideways or upside down. To fix this problem, you can use Photos to rotate the photo so that the subject appears right-side up. You can rotate a photo either clockwise or counterclockwise.

Rotate an Image

1 Open the image you want to rotate.

2 If you do not see the application bar, click the screen.

The application bar appears.

3 Click **Rotate** (⊙) until the image is the way you want it.

Photos saves your changes.

Delete an Image

The images that you create may not always turn out perfectly. A photo may be blurry, or an edited image may not turn out the way that you want it to.

When you are viewing an album or watching a slide show, having a bad image can make the experience less pleasant. You can prevent that from happening by deleting an image you no longer want to work with or view. You can delete a single image or multiple images with a single command.

Delete an Image

1 Open the image you want to delete.

2 If you do not see the application bar, click the screen.

The application bar appears.

3 Click **Delete** (🗑).

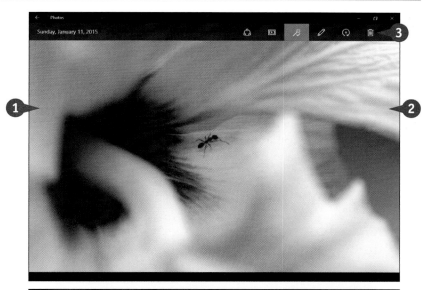

Photos asks you to confirm the deletion.

4 Click **Delete**.

Photos deletes the selected image or images.

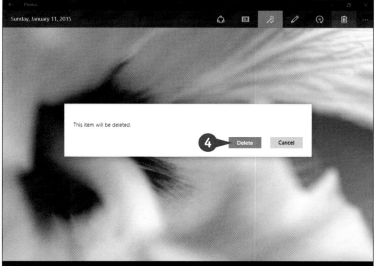

Print an Image

You can print an image from the Pictures library, or from any subfolder in the Pictures library. When you activate the Print command, the Print Pictures dialog box appears. You can use this dialog box to choose a printer and a layout, and to send the image to the printer.

You can print a single image or multiple images. If you work with multiple images, you can print them individually or print two or more images per sheet.

Print an Image

1 Open the image you want to print.

2 If you do not see the application bar, click the screen.

The application bar appears.

3 Click **More** (●●●).

Photos displays more commands.

4 Click **Print**.

The Print pane appears.

Ⓐ Photos displays a preview of the printout.

❺ Click ⌄ and click the printer you want to use.

❻ Select the number of copies you want.

❼ Click ⌄ and select the orientation of the photo.

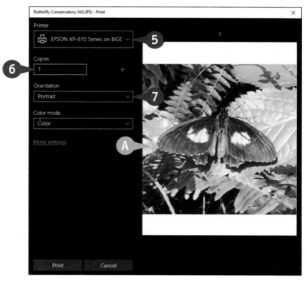

Ⓑ If you want to set extra options such as the paper size, paper type, or printout quality you prefer, click **More settings**.

❽ Click **Print**.

Photos sends your image to the printer.

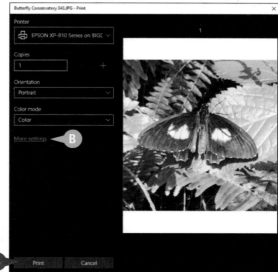

TIPS

Which orientation should I use?
The orientation determines how Photos lays out the image on the page. If your image has a greater height than width, choose Portrait; if your image has a greater width than height, choose Landscape.

What type of paper should I use for my photo printouts?
You can purchase a variety of photo-quality paper types for printing your digital photographs. Photo-quality paper, though more expensive than multipurpose paper, is designed to create a more permanent image and improve the resolution and color of the printed image. Photo-quality paper comes in glossy and matte finishes. Be sure to select a photo-quality paper that your printer manufacturer recommends.

Take a Picture with Your PC Camera

If your PC comes with a built-in camera or if you have an external camera attached to your PC, you can use the camera to take a picture of yourself, someone else, your surroundings — anything you want — using the Camera app.

The Camera app also gives you the option of recording a video. The Camera app stores each photo or video in a new album called *Camera Roll*, which appears in your Pictures library.

Take a Picture with Your PC Camera

1 In the taskbar's Search box, type **camera**.

2 Click **Camera**.

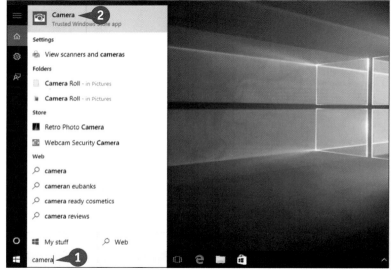

The first time that you start the Camera app, it asks for permission to use your location.

3 Click **Yes**.

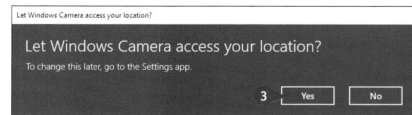

The Camera app loads.

Ⓐ A live feed from the camera appears.

Ⓑ If you want to adjust settings before taking the photo, click **More** (⬛) and then click **Settings**.

④ When you are ready to take the photo, click **Photo** (📷).

Ⓒ If you want to record a video instead, click **Video** (📹).

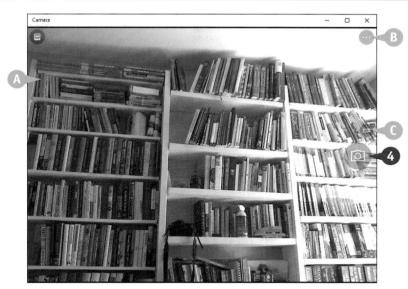

The Camera app takes the photo or starts the recording.

⑤ If you are recording a video, click **Video** (📹) again when you are finished.

The Camera app saves your photo or video.

TIPS

I accidentally clicked Block when I first started the Camera app. How can I change this?
Click **Start** (⊞) and then click **Settings**. Click **Privacy** and then click the **Webcam** tab. Click the **Camera** switch to **On**.

My video recordings take up lots of space. Can I fix this?
Yes, you can switch to a lower resolution, a lower frame rate, or both. Click **Settings** and then open the Resolution list in the Video section. The default resolution is 640 × 480, but you can select a smaller resolution such as 320 × 240. Similarly, the default frame rate is 30 frames per second (fps), but you can switch to a frame rate of 15fps or 12fps to save space.

Working with Multimedia

If you are into movies, TV shows, or music, you will appreciate the Windows apps that help you play, organize, edit, and generally get the most out of your multimedia. This chapter gives you the details on all the Windows media apps.

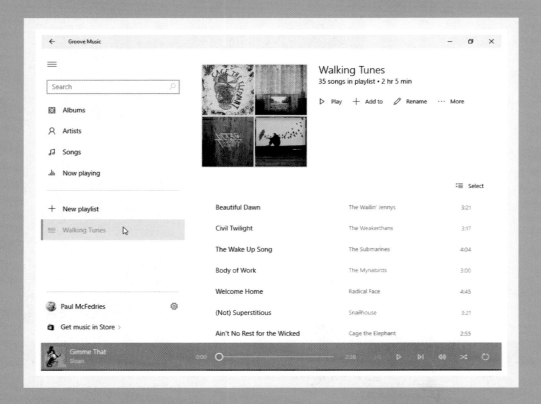

Import Videos from a Digital Camera

You can import videos from a digital camera and save them on your computer. If your camera stores the videos on a memory card, you can also use a memory card reader attached to your PC to upload the digital videos from the removable drive that Windows sets up when you insert the card.

To perform the import directly from your digital camera, you need a cable to connect your camera to your PC. Most digital cameras come with a USB cable. After you have the digital videos on your system, you can view them.

Import Videos from a Digital Camera

1 Plug in your camera or memory storage card reader.

Note: If you see a notification, click the notification and then skip to step **5**.

2 Click **File Explorer** (📁).

3 Click **This PC**.

File Explorer displays a list of the devices attached to your PC.

4 Right-click your digital camera.

5 Click **Import pictures and videos**.

The Import Pictures and Videos dialog box appears.

6 Click **Review, organize, and group items to import** (○ changes to ⦿).

A To make sure your videos are imported into the Videos library, click **More options** and follow the instructions in the first Tip.

7 Click **Next**.

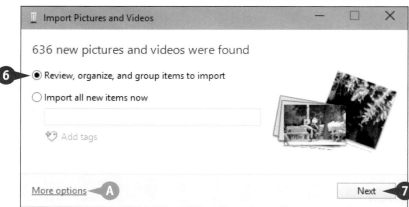

Windows displays the photos and videos that are on your camera.

Ⓑ Videos are indicated with a filmstrip graphic.

⑧ Click each video that you want to import (☐ changes to ☑).

Ⓒ If a group contains both photos and videos, click the group's **View all** link, and then click just the videos (☐ changes to ☑).

⑨ Type a name for each video import.

⑩ Click **Import**.

Windows imports the videos.

When the import is complete, File Explorer displays your imported videos.

Ⓓ Windows stores the imported videos in a folder named after today's date.

How do I ensure my videos are imported into the Videos library?

Follow steps **1** to **5** to open the Import Pictures and Videos dialog box and then click **More options**. Click the **Import videos to** ⌄ and then click **Videos**. Click **OK**.

How can I get my imported videos to appear in the Movies & TV app?

In the Search box, type **movies** and then click the **Movies & TV** app. Click **Settings** (⚙), click **Choose where we look for videos**, and click **Add** (➕). Click the folder that Windows created when you imported your videos, click **Add this folder to Videos**, and then click **Done**.

Navigate the Videos Library

Before you can work with your videos, you need to locate them on your PC. You do that by using the Movies & TV app to open the Videos library, which is a special folder designed specifically for storing digital videos, movies, and TV shows.

To get more out of the Videos library, you need to know the basic techniques for opening any videos that you have stored in it. If you are looking for commercial movies or TV shows, you can also use the Movies & TV app to buy or rent a movie or to buy a TV show episode.

Navigate the Videos Library

1 Click **Start** (⊞).

2 Click **Movies & TV**.

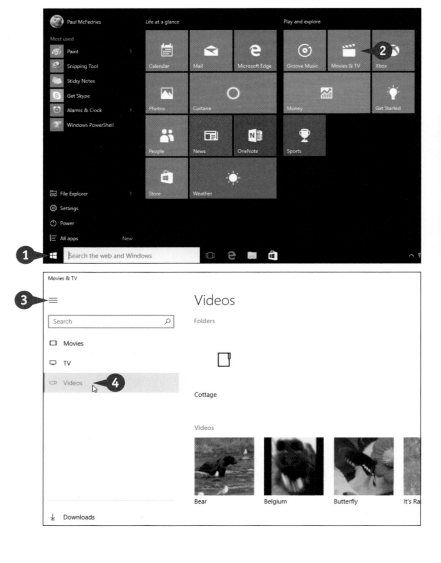

The Movies & TV app loads.

3 Click **Menu** (≡).

4 Click **Videos**.

The Movies & TV app displays the videos on your PC.

5 If the Video library contains one or more folders, click a folder.

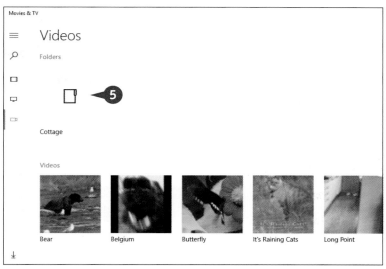

A The Movies & TV app displays the digital videos in the selected folder.

B You can click **Back** (←) to return to the previous section of the Movies & TV app.

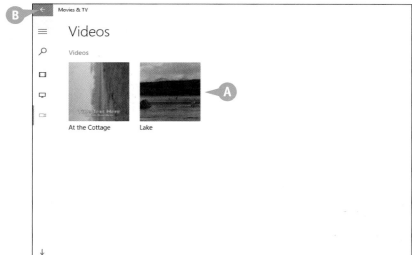

TIPS

How can I get my Camera app videos to appear in the Movies & TV app?

Open the Movies & TV app, click **Settings** (⚙), click **Preferences**, click **Choose where we look for videos**, click **Add** (⊞), select the **Pictures** folder, click **Camera Roll**, click **Add this folder to Videos**, and then click **Done**.

How do I get movies and TV shows?

Click **Start** (⊞) and then click **Store** to open the Store app, and then click **Movies & TV**. Click a movie or TV section heading (such as New Movies or Featured TV Shows); locate the movie, TV show season, or TV show episode; and then click either **Buy** or **Rent**.

Watch a Video

After you know how to use the Movies & TV app to navigate your Videos library, as shown in the previous section, "Navigate the Videos Library," you can use the app to select and play a video that you have on your PC. The Movies & TV app plays the video full screen on your PC, so you get the best viewing experience. When you have the video playing, you can pause and restart the playback, and you can use a special tool called the *scrubber* to quickly fast-forward or rewind the video to the spot that you want.

Watch a Video

Start a Video

1 In the Movies & TV app, locate the video you want to play.

2 Click the video.

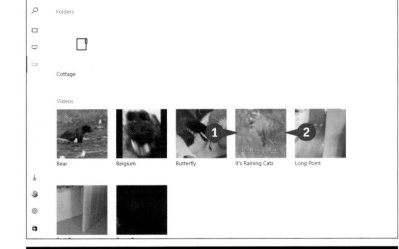

The Movies & TV app begins playing the video.

Control the Video Playback

1 Click the screen.

The Movies & TV app displays the playback controls.

A You can click **Pause** (||) to stop and restart the playback.

B You can click and drag the scrubber to rewind or fast-forward the video.

C You can click the timeline to jump to that position in the video.

TIP

How do I play a movie or TV show that I purchased or rented from the Windows Store?
After your purchase or rental has been downloaded to your PC, it appears in the Movies & TV app. Click **Start** (⊞) and then click **Movies & TV** to open the Movies & TV app. To watch a movie, click **Menu** (≡), click **Movies**, and then click the movie you want to view. To watch a TV show, click **Menu** (≡), click **TV**, and then click the episode you want to view.

Play a Music CD

You can play music CDs in Windows Media Player. When you first insert an audio disc in your PC's optical drive (that is, a drive capable of reading CDs and DVDs), Windows asks what action you want to perform with audio CDs, and you can tell it to play them using Windows Media Player.

The CD appears in the Now Playing window, and if you have an Internet connection you see the name of each track as well as other track data. You can control some playback options using the Now Playing window, but you can also switch to the Media Player library for more options.

Play a Music CD

Play a CD

1 Insert a music CD into your computer's optical drive.

A Windows displays an audio CD notification.

2 Click the notification.

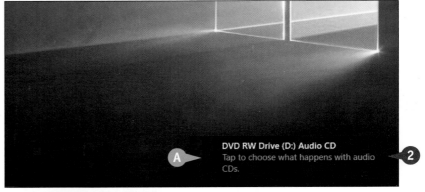

Windows displays a list of actions you can take when you insert an audio CD.

3 Click **Play audio CD**.

Note: If you see the Welcome to Windows Media Player dialog box, click **Recommended settings** (○ changes to ◉) and then click **Finish**.

The Windows Media Player Now Playing window appears and begins playing the audio CD.

Skip a Track

④ Click **Next** (▶▶◦) to skip to the next track.

⑤ Click **Previous** (◦◀◀) to skip to the previous track.

Pause and Resume Play

⑥ Click **Pause** (❚❚).

Windows Media Player pauses playback.

⑦ Click **Play** (▶).

Windows Media Player resumes playback where you left off.

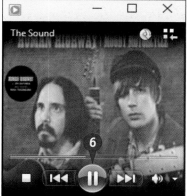

TIPS

Can I change the CD's audio levels?
Yes, Windows Media Player has a graphic equalizer component you can work with. To display it, right-click the **Now Playing** window, click **Enhancements**, and then click **Graphic equalizer**. To choose a predefined set of levels, click **Default** and then click a preset value such as Rock or Classical. Alternatively, you can use the sliders to set your own audio levels.

Can I display something other than album art during playback?
Yes. Right-click the **Now Playing** window and then click **Visualizations** to see a list of visualization categories. Click a category and then click the visualization you want to view.

continued ▶

Play a Music CD (continued)

You can use the playback buttons at the bottom of the Windows Media Player library to control how a CD plays. For example, you can easily switch from one song to another on the CD. You can also use the Repeat feature to tell Windows Media Player to start the CD over from the beginning after it has finished playing the CD. Windows Media Player also offers the Shuffle feature, which plays the CD's tracks in random order. If you want to learn how to import music from the CD to Windows Media Player, see the next section, "Copy Tracks from a Music CD."

Play a Music CD (continued)

Stop Play

8️⃣ Click **Stop** (■).

Windows Media Player stops playback.

If you click **Play** (▶) after clicking **Stop** (■), the current song starts over again.

9️⃣ Click **Switch to Library** (▦) to open the Windows Media Player library window.

The Windows Media Player library window opens.

Play Another Song

🔟 In the details pane, double-click the song you want to play.

Windows Media Player begins playing the song.

Ⓐ This area displays the current song title, the album title, and the song composer (if one is listed).

Repeat the CD

11 Click **Turn Repeat On** (⟳).

Windows Media Player restarts the CD after the last track finishes playing.

Note: To turn on Repeat from the Now Playing window, press Ctrl + T.

Play Songs Randomly

12 Click **Turn Shuffle On** (⤬).

Windows Media Player shuffles the order of play.

Note: To turn on Shuffle from the Now Playing window, press Ctrl + H.

TIPS

Why does my details pane not list the song titles?
Windows Media Player tries to gather information about the album from the Internet. If it cannot ascertain song titles, it displays track numbers instead. To add your own titles, right-click each song title you want to change, click **Edit**, type your text, and press Enter.

Can I keep the Now Playing window in view at all times?
Yes. You can configure the Now Playing window so that it stays on top of any other window that you have open on your desktop. Right-click the Now Playing window and then click **Always show Now Playing on top**.

Copy Tracks from a Music CD

You can add tracks from a music CD to the library in Windows Media Player. This enables you to listen to an album without having to put the CD into your optical drive each time. The process of adding tracks from a CD is called *copying*, or *ripping*, in Windows.

You can either rip an entire CD directly from the Now Playing window, or rip selected tracks using the library. You can also use the tracks to create your own playlists and to create your own custom CDs.

Copy Tracks from a Music CD

Rip an Entire CD Using the Now Playing Window

1. Insert a CD into your computer's optical drive.

 The Now Playing window appears.

2. Click **Rip CD** ().

 Windows Media Player begins ripping the entire CD.

Rip Selected Tracks Using the Library

1. Insert a CD into your computer's optical drive.

 If the Now Playing window appears, click **Switch to Library** (⊞).

 🅐 Windows Media Player displays a list of the CD's tracks.

2. Click the CD tracks that you do not want to copy (☑ changes to ☐).

3. Click **Rip CD**.

Windows Media Player begins copying the track or tracks.

B The Rip Status column displays the copy progress.

C After each file is copied, the Rip Status column displays a Ripped to library message.

D The copy is complete when all the tracks you selected display the Ripped to library status.

How do I remove a track from the library?

In the library, click **Music**, click **Album**, and then double-click the album that you ripped to display a list of the tracks. Right-click the track that you want to remove and then click **Delete**.

Can I adjust the quality of the copies?

Yes, by changing the *bit rate*, which is a measure of how much of the CD's original data is copied to your computer. This is measured in kilobits per second (Kbps); the higher the value, the higher the quality, but the more hard drive space each track takes up. Click **Rip Settings**, click **Audio Quality**, and then click the value you want.

Navigate the Music Library

Before you can work with your songs and albums, you need to locate them on your PC. You do that by using the Groove Music app to open the Windows Music library, which is a special folder designed specifically for storing digital music.

To get more out of the Music library, you need to know the basic techniques for opening any albums that you have stored in it. You can also use the Groove Music app to purchase commercial albums or songs.

Navigate the Music Library

1 Click **Start** (⊞).

2 Click **Groove Music**.

The Groove Music app loads.

3 Click **Menu** (≡).

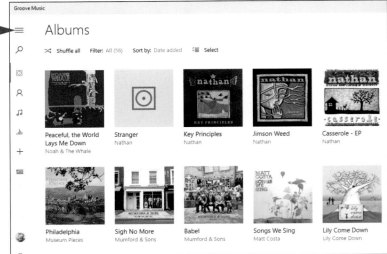

The Music library appears.

④ Click a music category.

Ⓐ The music in that category appears.

⑤ Click a category item.

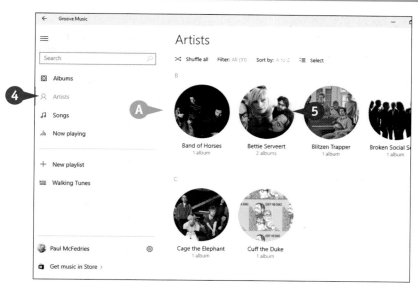

Ⓑ If the category item contains multiple subitems, Music displays those subitems.

Ⓒ You can click **Back** (←) to return to the previous section of the Groove Music app.

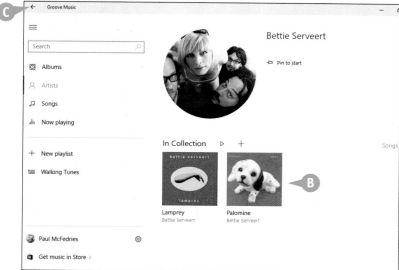

What if a song that I want to play does not appear in the Music library?

If your song is outside the Music library, the Groove Music app does not see it. Click **Settings** (⚙), click **Preferences**, click **Choose where we look for music on this PC**, and click **Add** (➕). Locate and click the folder that contains your music, and then click **Add this folder to Music**.

How do I buy an album?

Click **Start** (⊞) and then click **Store** to open the Store app, and then click **Music**. Either use the Search box to look for the artist or album title, or click a section heading, and locate the album. Click the album and then click the price button.

Play Music

If you want to listen to music while using your PC, and your PC has either built-in or connected speakers, you can use the Groove Music app to play tunes from your Music library. You can listen to all the songs on an album, all the songs from a particular artist, or individual songs.

The Groove Music app offers several features for controlling the music playback. You can also play albums, artists, and songs in random order and play albums and artists repeatedly.

Play Music

Start Music

1 Use the Groove Music app to display your music.

Note: See the previous section, "Navigate the Music Library," for details.

2 Click the item that contains the music you want to play.

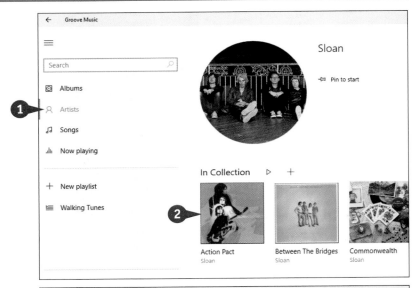

The Groove Music app opens the item and displays a list of songs.

3 Click **Play** (▷).

Ⓐ You can also click a song and then click **Play** (▷).

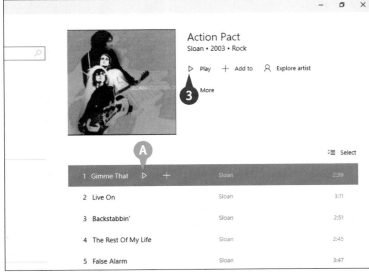

Control the Music Playback

Ⓑ When you play music, the Groove Music app displays the playback controls.

Ⓒ You can click **Pause** (❙❙) to stop and restart the playback.

Ⓓ You can click and drag the scrubber to rewind or fast-forward the current song.

Ⓔ To control the volume, you can click **Volume** (🔊) and then click and drag the slider.

Ⓕ You can click **Next** (▶❙) to jump to the next song.

Ⓖ You can click **Previous** (❙◀) to return to the beginning of the current song; click **Previous** (❙◀) again to jump to the previous song.

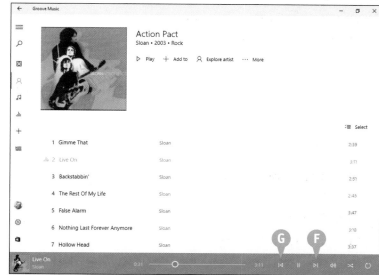

TIPS

Is there a way to get an album to automatically start over from the beginning?

Yes, the Groove Music app offers a Repeat feature that automatically restarts the current album from the beginning as soon as the album ends. To activate this feature, start playing the album and then click **Repeat** (🔁).

How do I play an album's or artist's songs randomly?

You need to activate the Shuffle feature, which plays the songs for the current album or artist in random order. To activate this feature, start playing the album or artist and then click **Shuffle** (🔀).

Create a Playlist

A *playlist* is a collection of songs that represents a subset of your total music collection. A playlist can include audio tracks you ripped from a music CD, songs downloaded from the Internet, or music purchased through the Xbox Music Store.

You can use the Groove Music app to create customized playlists that include only the songs you want to hear. For example, you might want to create a playlist of upbeat or festive songs to play during a party or celebration. Similarly, you might want to create a playlist of your current favorite songs to play during a workout.

Create a Playlist

① Click **Menu** (☰).

② Click **New playlist**.

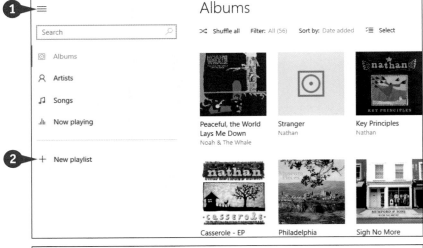

Music prompts you to name the new playlist.

③ Type a name for the new playlist.

④ Click **Save**.

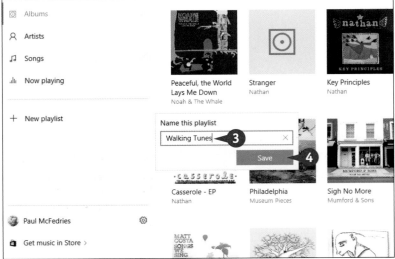

5 Click a song that you want to add to the playlist.

6 Click **Add** (➕).

7 Click the name of your playlist.

Music adds the song to the playlist.

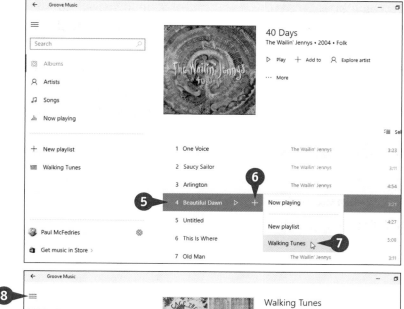

8 Click **Menu** (≡).

9 Click the playlist.

Ⓐ Music displays a list of the songs you added.

10 Click **Play** (▷) to listen to the playlist.

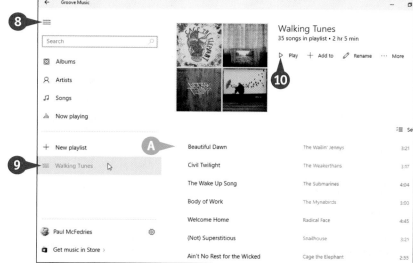

TIPS

How do I make changes to an existing playlist?
Click the playlist to open it. To change the playlist name, click **Edit** (✐), type the new playlist name, and then click **Save**. To change the song order, click and drag songs up and down, or right-click a song and then click either **Move up** or **Move down**. To delete a song from the playlist, right-click the song and then click **Remove from playlist**.

How do I delete a playlist?
Click the playlist to open it, click **More** (···), and then click **Delete**. When Music asks you to confirm, click **Delete**.

Switch Between PC Speakers and Headphones

I f you have connected a pair of headphones to your PC, you can use those headphones to listen to music or to hear the sound from videos, TV shows, and movies. If you want to listen through your PC's built-in sound system instead, you must disable the headphones by disconnecting them. To avoid that hassle, you can leave your headphones connected and use Control Panel's Sound feature to switch between sound output devices.

Switch Between PC Speakers and Headphones

1 In the Search box, type **control**.

2 Click **Control Panel**.

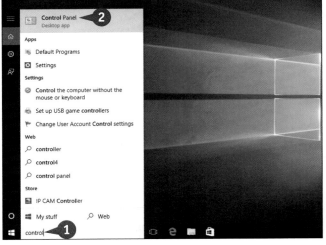

The Control Panel appears.

3 Click **Hardware and Sound**.

The Hardware and Sound window appears.

④ Click **Manage audio devices**.

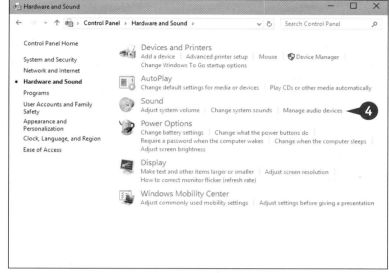

The Sound dialog box appears with the Playback tab selected.

⑤ Click the audio device you want to use for the sound playback.

⑥ Click **Set Default**.

⑦ Click **OK**.

Windows now uses the device you set as the default for sound playback.

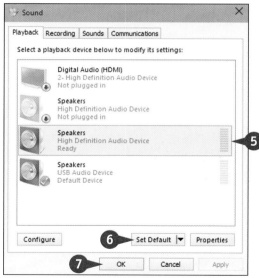

TIPS

I am hard of hearing in one ear. How do I turn up the headphone sound for that ear?
Follow steps **1** to **4**, click your headphones, click **Properties**, click the **Levels** tab, and then click **Balance**. In the Balance dialog box, drag the slider marked either L (left) or R (right) to the level you prefer and then click **OK**.

How can I prevent wide fluctuations in volume between the different media that I play?
Activate the Loudness Equalization feature, which makes all your PC's sounds equally loud. Follow steps **1** to **4**, click your headphones, click **Properties**, click the **Enhancements** tab, click **Loudness Equalization** (☐ changes to ☑), and then click **OK**.

CHAPTER 9

Editing
Documents

To be productive with Windows, you need to know how to work with documents. In this chapter, you learn how to create, save, open, and work with documents and OneNote notebooks.

Create and Save a Document

When you are ready to create something using Windows, in most cases you begin by launching a program and then using that program to create a new document to hold your work. Many Windows programs (such as WordPad and Paint) create a new document for you automatically when you begin the program. However, you can also use these programs to create another new document after you have started the program.

After you create a document and make any changes to it, you must save the document to preserve your work.

Create and Save a Document

Create a New Document

1. Click **File**.

2. Click **New**.

 The program creates the new document.

Note: In most programs, you can also press `Ctrl`+`N` to create a new document.

Save a Document

1. Click **File**.

2. Click **Save**.

Note: In most programs, you can also press `Ctrl`+`S` or click Save (🖫).

Note: If you saved the document previously, your changes are now preserved. You do not need to follow the rest of the steps in this section.

If this is a new document that you have never saved before, the Save As dialog box appears.

3 Click **Documents**.

Note: In most programs, the Documents library is selected automatically when you save a document.

A Windows opens the Documents library.

4 Click in the File Name text box and type the name you want to use for the document.

Note: The name you type can be up to 255 characters long, but it cannot include the following characters: < > , ? : " \ *.

5 Click **Save**.

The app saves your document in the folder you specified.

TIPS

Why do I need to save a document?

As you work on a document, Windows stores the changes in your computer's memory. However, Windows erases your PC's memory whenever you shut down or restart the computer. Without saving, you would lose all the changes you have made to your document. Saving the document preserves your changes on your computer's hard drive.

Do I have to save all my files to the Documents library?

No. You can create a subfolder within Documents. In the Save As dialog box, click **New folder**, type the name of the folder, press **Enter**, double-click the new folder, and then follow steps **4** and **5**.

Open a Document

To work with a document that you have saved in the past, you typically need to open the document in the program that you used to create it. When you save a document, you save its contents to your PC's hard drive, and those contents are stored in a separate file. When you open the document using the same application that you used to save it, Windows loads the file's contents into memory and displays the document in the application. You can then view or edit the document as needed.

Open a Document

1 Start the program you want to work with.

2 Click **File**.

A If you see the document you want in a list of the most recently used documents on the File menu, click the name to open it. You can then skip the rest of the steps in this section.

3 Click **Open**.

Note: In most programs, you can also press Ctrl + O or click **Open** ().

The Open dialog box appears.

4 Click **Documents**.

Note: In most programs, the Documents library is selected automatically when you open a document.

B If you want to open the document from some other folder, click here, click your username, and then double-click the folder.

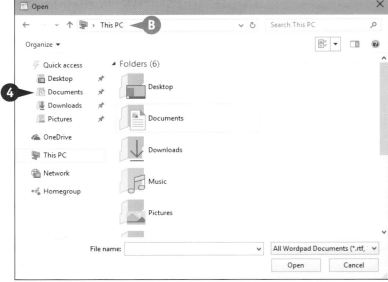

C Windows opens the Documents library.

5 Click the document name.

6 Click **Open**.

D The document appears in the program window.

TIPS

Is there a more direct way to open a document?
Yes, there is. You do not always need to open the program first. Instead, use File Explorer to open the folder that contains the document and then double-click the document. Windows automatically launches the program and opens the document.

Is there a quick way to locate a document?
Yes, Windows offers a documents search feature, which is handy if your Documents library contains many files. Use the taskbar's Search box to type some or all of the document's filename, click **Search my stuff**, and then click the Documents tab.

Change the Text Font

You can add visual appeal to a document by changing the font formatting. The font formatting includes attributes such as the typeface, style, size, or special effects.

A *typeface* — also called a *font* — is a distinctive character design that you can apply to the selected text in a document. The *type style* refers to formatting applied to text, such as **bold** or *italics*. The *type size* refers to the height of each character, which is measured in *points*; 72 points equal one inch. *Special effects* are styles that change the appearance of the text, such as underline and ~~strikethrough~~.

Change the Text Font

1 Select the text you want to format.

2 Display the font options.

A In WordPad, you display the font options by clicking the **Home** tab.

Note: In many other programs, you display the font options by clicking **Format** in the menu bar and then clicking the **Font** command.

3 In the Font list, click ▼ and then click the typeface you want.

4 In the Size list, click ▼ and then click the type size you want.

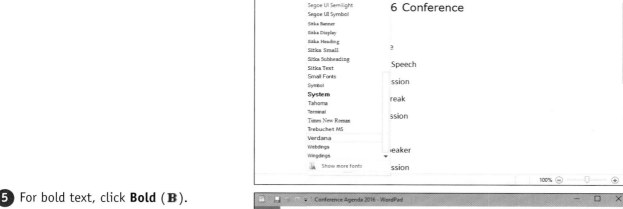

5 For bold text, click **Bold** (**B**).

6 For italics, click **Italic** (*I*).

7 For underlining, click **Underline** (U̲).

8 For color, click the **Font color** ▼ and then click a color.

Ⓑ The program applies the font formatting to the selected text.

Note: Here are some shortcuts that work in most programs: For bold, press Ctrl+B; for italics, press Ctrl+I; for underline, press Ctrl+U.

How can I make the best use of fonts in my documents?

- Use one or two typefaces to avoid the "ransom note" look.
- Avoid overly decorative typefaces because they are often difficult to read.
- Use bold only for document titles, subtitles, and headings.
- Use italics only to emphasize words and phrases, or for the titles of books and magazines.
- Use larger type sizes only for document titles, subtitles, and, possibly, headings.
- In general, dark text on a light background is the easiest to read.

Find Text

In large documents, when you need to find specific text, you can save a lot of time by using the program's Find feature. In short documents that contain only a few dozen or even a few hundred words, finding a specific word or phrase is usually not difficult. However, many documents contain hundreds or even thousands of words, so finding a word or phrase becomes much more difficult and time consuming.

You can work around this problem by using the Find feature, which searches the entire document in the blink of an eye. Most programs that work with text — including the Windows WordPad and Notepad programs — have the Find feature.

Find Text

1 Click **Find**.

A In WordPad, you display the Editing options by clicking the **Home** tab.

Note: In many programs, you run the Find command by clicking **Edit** in the menu bar and then clicking the **Find** command, or by pressing `Ctrl` + `F`.

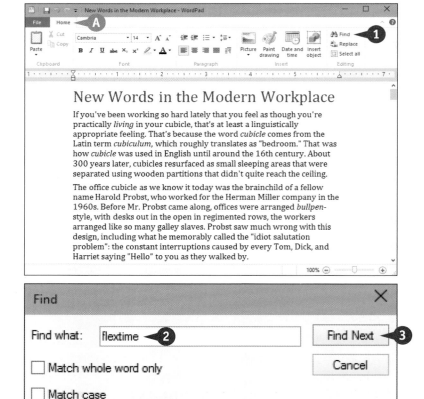

The Find dialog box appears.

2 Click in the Find What text box and type the text you want to find.

3 Click **Find Next**.

B The program selects the next instance of the search text.

Note: If the search text does not exist in the document, the program displays a dialog box to let you know.

4 If the selected instance is not the one you want, click **Find Next** until the program finds the correct instance.

5 Click **Close** (✕) to close the Find dialog box.

C The program leaves the found text selected.

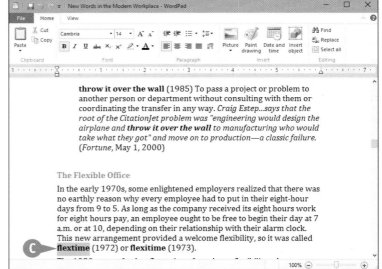

A search for a word such as *the* also matches larger words such as *theme* and *bother*. How can I avoid this?
In the Find dialog box, click **Match whole word only** (☐ changes to ☑). This tells the program to match the search text only if it is a word on its own.

A search for a name such as *Bill* also matches the non-name *bill*. How do I fix this?
In the Find dialog box, click **Match case** (☐ changes to ☑). This tells the program to match the search text only if it has the same mix of uppercase and lowercase letters that you specify in the Find What text box.

Replace Text

You can make it easier to replace multiple instances of one word with another by taking advantage of the program's Replace feature. Do you need to replace a word or part of a word with some other text? If you have several instances to replace, you can save time and do a more accurate job if you let the program's Replace feature replace the word for you. Most programs that work with text — including the Windows WordPad and Notepad programs — have the Replace feature.

Replace Text

1 Click **Replace**.

Ⓐ In WordPad, you display the Editing options by clicking the **Home** tab.

Note: In many programs, you run the Replace command by clicking **Edit** in the menu bar and then clicking the **Replace** command, or by pressing **Ctrl** + **H**.

The Replace dialog box appears.

2 Click in the Find What text box, and type the text you want to find.

3 Click in the Replace With text box, and type the text you want to use as the replacement.

4 Click **Find Next**.

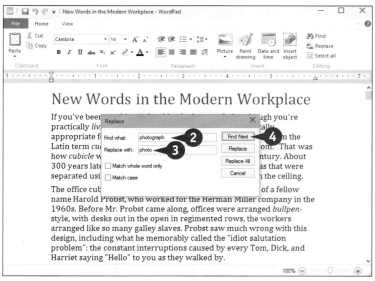

ⓑ The program selects the next instance of the search text.

Note: If the search text does not exist in the document, the program displays a dialog box to let you know.

❺ If the selected instance is not the one you want, click **Find Next** until the program finds the correct instance.

❻ Click **Replace**.

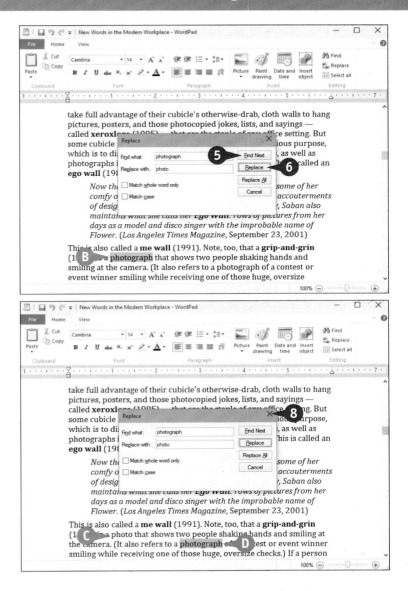

ⓒ The program replaces the selected text with the replacement text.

ⓓ The program selects the next instance of the search text.

❼ Repeat steps **5** and **6** until you have replaced all the instances you want to replace.

❽ Click **Close** (✕) to close the Replace dialog box.

TIP

Is there a faster way to replace every instance of the search text with the replacement text?
Yes. In the Replace dialog box, click **Replace All**. This tells the program to replace every instance of the search text with the replacement text. However, you should exercise some caution with this feature because it may make some replacements that you did not intend. Click **Find Next** a few times to make sure the matches are correct. Also, consider clicking **Match whole word only** and **Match case** (☐ changes to ☑), as described in the section "Find Text," earlier in this chapter.

Insert Special Symbols

Yaou can make your documents more readable and more useful by inserting special symbols that are not available via your keyboard. The keyboard is home to a large number of letters, numbers, and symbols. However, the keyboard is missing some useful characters. For example, it is missing the foreign characters in words such as café and Köln. Similarly, your writing might require mathematical symbols such as ÷ and ½, financial symbols such as ¢ and ¥, or commercial symbols such as © and ®. These and many more symbols are available in Windows via the Character Map program.

Insert Special Symbols

1. In the Search box, type **char**.
2. Click **Character Map**.

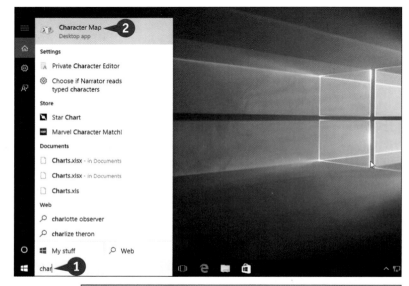

The Character Map window appears.

3. Click the symbol you want.
4. Click **Select**.

Ⓐ Character Map adds the symbol to the Characters to Copy text box.

5. Click **Copy**.
6. Click **Close** (✕) to shut down Character Map after you choose all the characters you want.

7 In your document, position the cursor where you want to insert the symbol.

B In WordPad, you can display the Clipboard options by clicking the **Home** tab.

8 Click **Paste**.

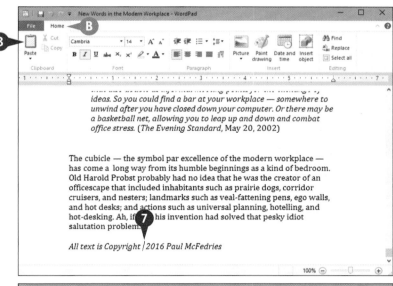

C The program inserts the symbol.

When I click a symbol, Character Map sometimes displays a "keystroke" in the status bar. What does this mean?

This tells you that you can insert the symbol directly into your document by pressing the keystroke shown. For example, you can insert the copyright symbol (©) by pressing Alt + 0 1 6 9. When you type the numbers, be sure to use your keyboard's numeric keypad.

Are there even more symbols available?

Yes, dozens of extra symbols are available in the Character Map program's Webdings and Wingdings typefaces. To see these symbols, click the Font list ▼ and then click either **Webdings** or **Wingdings**.

Make a Copy of a Document

When you need to create a document that is nearly identical to an existing document, instead of creating the new document from scratch, you can save time by making a copy of the existing document and then modifying the copy as needed. For example, you might have a résumé cover letter that you want to modify for a different job application. Similarly, this year's conference agenda is likely to be similar to last year's. Instead of creating these new documents from scratch, it is much faster to copy the original document and then edit the copy as needed.

Make a Copy of a Document

1 Start the program you want to work with and open the original document.

2 Click **File**.

3 Click **Save as**.

The Save As dialog box appears.

4 Click **Documents**.

Note: In most programs, the Documents library is selected automatically when you run the Save As command.

A Windows opens the Documents library.

5 Click in the File Name text box and type the name you want to use for the copy.

Note: The name you type can be up to 255 characters long, but it cannot include the following characters: < > , ? : " \ *.

6 Click **Save**.

The program closes the original document and opens the copy you just created.

B The filename you typed appears in the program's title bar.

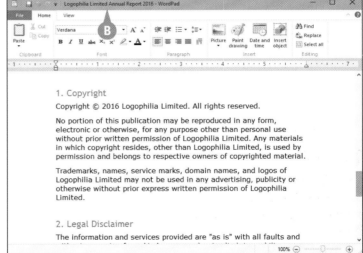

TIP

Can I use the Save As command to make a backup copy of a document?
Yes, Save As can operate as a rudimentary backup procedure. (To learn more about keeping a history of your files, see Chapter 14.) Create a copy with the same name as the original, but store the copy in a different location. Good places to choose are a second hard drive, a USB flash drive, or a memory card. Remember, too, that after you complete the Save As steps, the *backup copy* will be open in the program. Be sure to close the copy and then reopen the original.

Create a OneNote Notebook

You can use the OneNote app to record and save miscellaneous bits of information, including text, lists, drawings, images, web pages, and tables of data. All of this is stored in a special file called a *notebook*. Within each notebook you can organize your data within *sections*, where each section is devoted to a particular subject. Each section is then divided into one or more *pages*, and you use these pages to enter your data.

Note that your Windows user account must be connected to a Microsoft account to use OneNote.

Create a OneNote Notebook

1 Click **Start** (▦).

2 Click **OneNote**.

3 The first time you start OneNote, the app takes you through a few introductory screens (not shown). On each screen, click **Next** (>) to continue.

4 Click **Start using OneNote**.

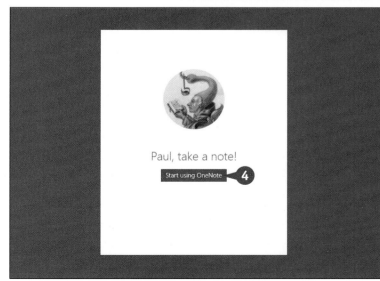

The OneNote app appears.

5 Click the screen.

6 Type a name for the notebook.

7 Press Enter.

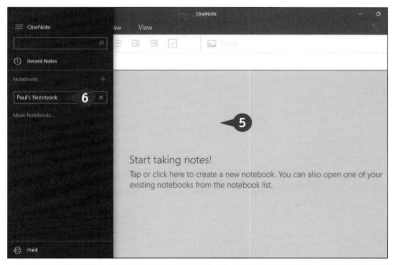

OneNote creates a new notebook and populates it with a single section and page.

A You can click **Menu** (≡) to hide the OneNote sidebar.

B To name the section, you can right-click it, click **Rename Section**, and then type the name.

C You can click here to add a title for the page.

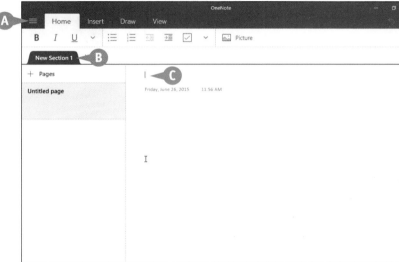

TIPS

Can I create more than one notebook?
Yes, you can add more notebooks if you have data to keep separate. Click **Menu** (≡), click **Add** (+) to the right of the Notebooks heading, type a name for the new notebook, and then press Enter.

Can I delete a notebook?
Yes, but you cannot delete a notebook using the OneNote app. Instead, you must use the online version of OneNote. Log in to http://onedrive.live.com. Click **Documents**, position the mouse (⇩) over the OneNote notebook, and then click the file's check box (☐ changes to ☑). Click **Manage** and then click **Delete**.

Add Pages and Sections to a Notebook

Y ou can keep your notes organized and easy to find by taking advantage of OneNote's pages and
sections. Each OneNote notebook consists of one or more sections, which you use to break down
the notebook's overall topic or theme into smaller, more manageable subjects.

You can further break down each section into one or more pages, which are the OneNote items
within which you add text, images, lists, and other data. You can add as many sections and pages as
you need to keep your notes organized.

Add Pages and Sections to a Notebook

Add a Page

1 Click the section in which you
want to add the page.

2 Click **Add** (**+**).

OneNote adds a page to the
section.

3 Type a title for the page and
press **Enter**.

OneNote sets the page title.

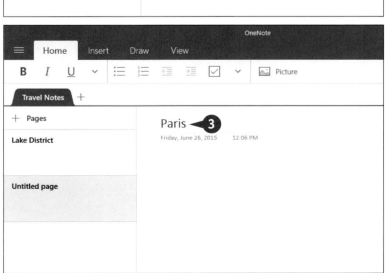

Add a Section

1 Click **Add** (**+**).

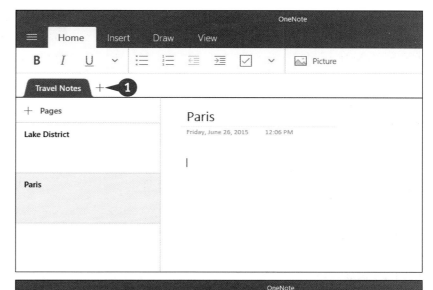

OneNote adds a section to the notebook.

2 Type the section name and press **Enter**.

OneNote sets the section title.

A OneNote adds a blank page to the new section.

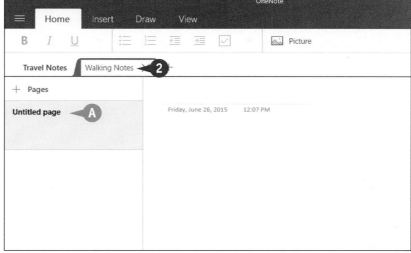

TIPS

How do I rename a section or change a section's color scheme?

To change the section name, right-click the section tab, click **Rename Section**, type the new name, and then press **Enter**. To change the section's color scheme, right-click the section tab, click **Section Color**, and then click the color you want to use.

How do I delete a page or section?

To delete a page, right-click the page in the Pages list, click **Delete Page**, and then click **Delete Page** to confirm. To delete a section, right-click the section tab, click **Delete Section**, and then click **Delete Section** to confirm.

Add Text Notes

Once you have your sections and pages, your next step is to fill your pages with content. OneNote makes it easy to insert everything from simple text notes to pictures to entire files. All OneNote content appears inside a *container*, which is essentially a box that surrounds the content. After you have some content inside a container, you can move the container around on the page, edit or format the container content, and more.

Most page content consists of text notes, and OneNote makes it very simple to add text to a page.

Add Text Notes

Add a Text Note

1 Click the section you want to use.

2 Click the page you want to use.

3 Click inside the page at the position where you want the text to appear.

Ⓐ OneNote adds an insertion point cursor.

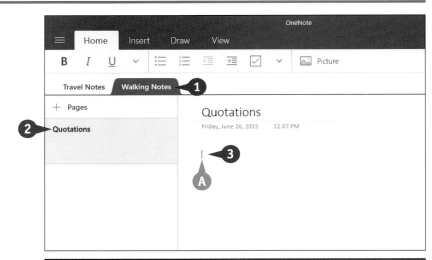

4 Type your text.

Ⓑ OneNote adds a container around your text.

5 When your text note is complete, click outside the container.

OneNote adds the text note to the page.

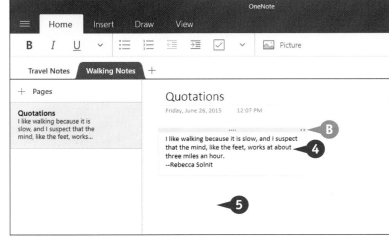

Size a Text Note Container

1 Position the mouse (⌖) over the right edge of the container (⌖ changes to ↔).

2 Click and drag the mouse (↔) right for a larger container, or left for a smaller container, and then release the mouse.

OneNote resizes the container and adjusts the text to fit the new size.

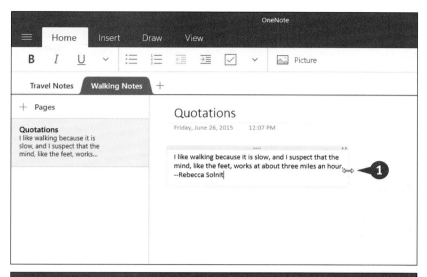

Move a Text Note Container

1 Position the mouse (⌖) over the middle of the top edge of the container (⌖ changes to ⊕).

2 Click and drag the mouse (⊕) to the position you want and then release the mouse.

OneNote moves the container to the new position.

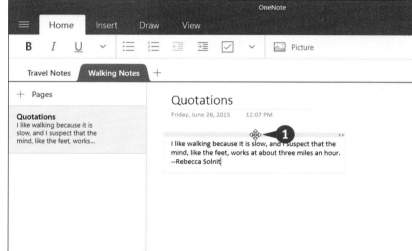

TIP

How do I format note text?

Select the note text you want to format and then click the **Home** tab to display the text note formatting options. You can click **Bold** (**B**), **Italic** (*I*), or **Underline** (*I*) to apply those font styles to the text. You can also click the **Font formatting** ⌄ to apply effects such as color, superscript, and strikethrough.

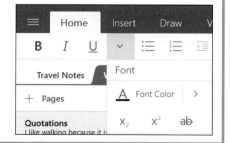

Add an Image to a Notebook Page

Although you will populate your OneNote notebooks mostly with text notes, you can also insert other types of content, including images. You can either insert an image file from your PC's hard drive or, if your computer has a camera attached, you can take a photo and insert it directly into the page. As with text notes, OneNote adds an image to the page within a container that you can move and size as needed.

Add an Image to a Notebook Page

1 Click the section you want to use.

2 Click the page you want to use.

3 Click inside the page at the position where you want the image to appear.

4 Click the **Insert** tab.

5 Click **Picture**.

The Open dialog box appears.

6 Click the image.

7 Click **Open**.

A OneNote inserts the image into the page.

B To work with the image, right-click it, click **Picture**, and then use the tools that appear.

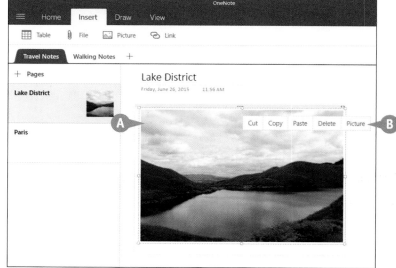

Work with Notebook Lists

Many OneNote notes consist of lists of items. If you have a list that does not require a particular sequence, you can add the items to a page as a bulleted list. If you have a list that does require a sequence, then you can add the items to the page as a numbered list instead.

One of the most common OneNote list types is the to-do list, which is a collection of tasks, each with a leading check box. When you complete a task, you activate its check box.

Work with Notebook Lists

Create a Bulleted or Numbered List

1 Click the section you want to use.

2 Click the page you want to use.

3 Click inside the page at the position where you want the list to appear.

4 Click the **Home** tab.

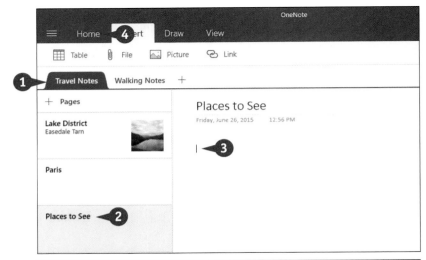

5 Click the type of list you want to add:

Ⓐ Click **Bulleted List** (☰) to create a list with bullets.

Ⓑ Click **Numbering** (☰) to create a list with numbers.

OneNote adds the list to a container.

6 Click inside the container and type your list items, pressing `Enter` after each item.

7 When you are done, click outside the container.

OneNote adds the list to the page.

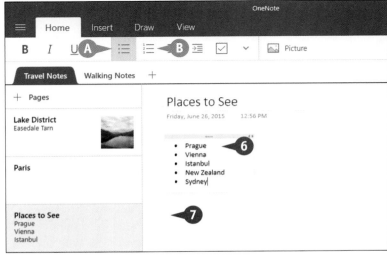

Create a To-Do List

1 Click the section you want to use.

2 Click the page you want to use.

3 Add the to-do list.

4 Select all the items in the list.

5 Click **Tag as To Do** (☑).

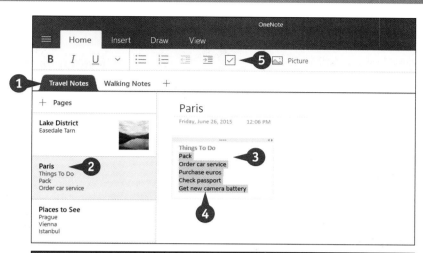

C OneNote adds a check box to the left of each item.

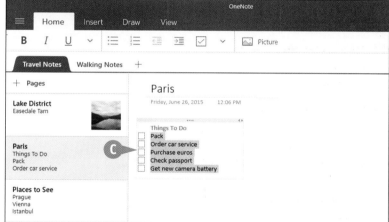

TIPS

Are there other tags I can apply to text?
Yes. OneNote offers six other tag types: Important, Question, Critical, Contact, Address, and Phone Number. To apply one of these tags, select the text, click **Home**, click the ⌄ to the right of **Tag as To Do** (☑), and then click the tag.

How do I create sub-bullets and subordinate numbered lists?
Select the bullet or numbered item that you want to convert. Click the **Home** tab and then click **Increase Indent** (⋲). OneNote converts a bullet to a sub-bullet that uses an unfilled icon; OneNote moves a numbered item to a subordinate list that uses lowercase letters.

Print a Document

When you need a hard copy of your document, either for your files or to distribute to someone else, you can get a hard copy by sending the document to your printer. Most applications that deal with documents also come with a Print command. When you run this command, the Print dialog box appears. You use the Print dialog box to choose the printer you want to use as well as to specify how many copies you want to print. Many Print dialog boxes also enable you to see a preview of your document before printing it.

Print a Document

1 Turn on your printer.

2 Open the document you want to print.

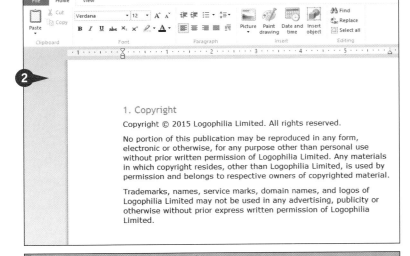

3 Click **File**.

4 Click **Print**.

Note: In many programs, you can select the Print command by pressing Ctrl+P or by clicking **Print** (🖨).

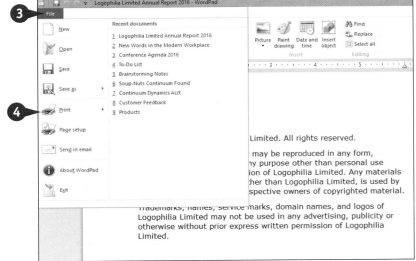

The Print dialog box appears.

Note: The layout of the Print dialog box varies from program to program. The WordPad version shown here is a typical example.

5 If you have more than one printer, click the printer you want to use.

6 Click the **Number of copies** ⬍ to specify the number of copies to print.

7 Click **Print**.

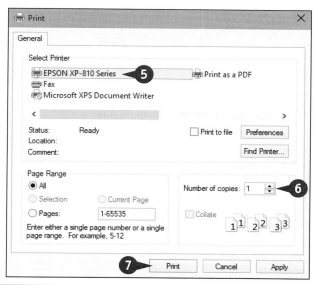

A Windows prints the document. The print icon (🖨) appears in the taskbar's notification area while the document prints.

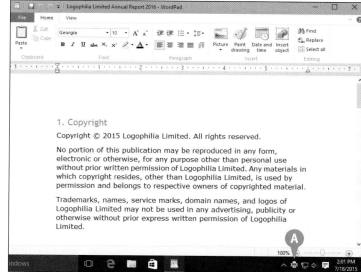

TIP

How do I print only part of a document?

Most programs support the following methods:

- Print selected text: Select the text and then, in the Print dialog box, click **Selection** (○ changes to ◉).
- Print a specific page: Place the cursor on the page and then, in the Print dialog box, click **Current Page** (○ changes to ◉).
- Print a range of pages: In the Print dialog box, click **Pages** (○ changes to ◉), type the first page number, a dash (–), and the last page number (for example, 1–5).

CHAPTER 10

Working with Files

This chapter shows you how to work with the files on your computer. These easy and efficient methods show you how to view, select, copy, move, rename, and delete files, as well as how to restore accidentally deleted files, how to extract files from a compressed folder, and more.

Select a File

Before you can use File Explorer to do any work with one or more files, you first have to select the files so that Windows knows which ones you want to work with. For example, before you can move files to a new location, you must first select the files you want to move. You can select just a single file, two or more files, or group of files, or all the files in a folder. Although you learn specifically about selecting files in this section, the technique for selecting folders is exactly the same.

Select a File

Select a Single File

1. Click **File Explorer** (📁).
2. Open the folder containing the file.
3. Click the file.

Select Multiple Files

1. Open the folder containing the files.
2. Click the first file you want to select.
3. Press and hold Ctrl and click each of the other files you want to select.

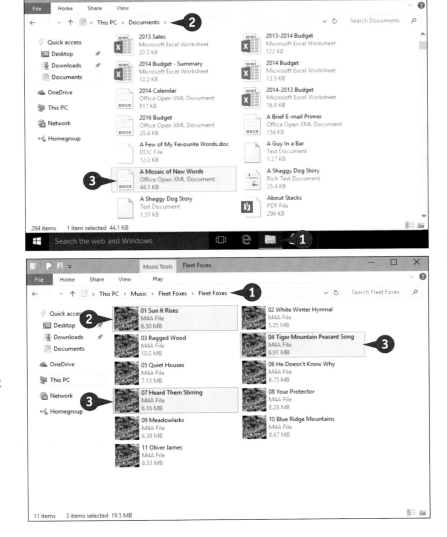

Select a Group of Files

1 Open the folder containing the files.

2 Position the mouse (◨) slightly above and slightly to the left of the first file in the group.

3 Click and drag the mouse (◨) down and to the right until all the files in the group are selected.

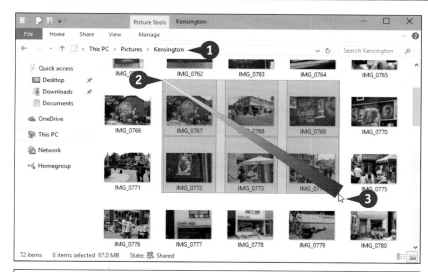

Select All Files

1 Open the folder containing the files.

2 Click the **Home** tab.

3 Click **Select all**.

Note: A quick way to select all the files in a folder is to press Ctrl + A.

A File Explorer selects all the files in the folder.

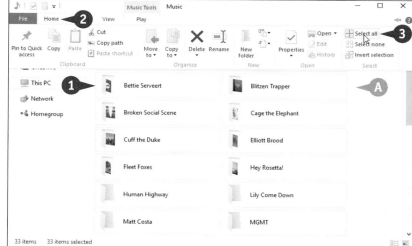

TIP

How do I deselect a file?

Depending on the situation, there are a few ways to deselect files:

- To deselect a single file from a multiple-file selection, press and hold Ctrl and click the file you want to deselect.

- To deselect all files, either click the **Home** tab and then click **Select none**, or click an empty area within the folder.

- To reverse the selection — deselect the selected files and select the deselected files — click the **Home** tab and then click **Invert selection**.

Change the File View

You can configure how Windows displays the files in a folder by changing the file view. This enables you to see larger or smaller icons or the details of each file.

You can choose a view such as Small Icons to see more files in the folder window. A view such as Large Icons or Extra Large Icons enables you to view images as thumbnail versions of each picture. If you want to see more information about the files, choose either the Tiles view or Details view.

Change the File View

1 In File Explorer, open the folder containing the files you want to view.

2 Click the **View** tab.

3 In the Layout section, click **More** ($\overline{\overline{\mathbf{\tau}}}$).

Windows displays the Layout gallery.

4 Click the view you want.

A File Explorer changes the file view (this example shows Tiles view).

Preview a File

Windows enables you to view the contents of some files without opening them. This makes it easier to select the file you want to work with because it means you do not have to run an application to see the file's contents. Previewing the file is faster and uses fewer system resources. Windows previews only certain types of files, such as text documents, rich text documents, web pages, images, and videos.

Preview a File

1 In File Explorer, open the folder containing the file you want to preview.

2 Click the **View** tab.

3 Click **Preview pane**.

Ⓐ The Preview pane appears.

4 Click a file.

Ⓑ The file's contents appear in the Preview pane.

Ⓒ You can click and drag the left border of the Preview pane to change its size.

Note: When you are finished with the Preview pane, you can click **Preview pane** on the View tab to close it.

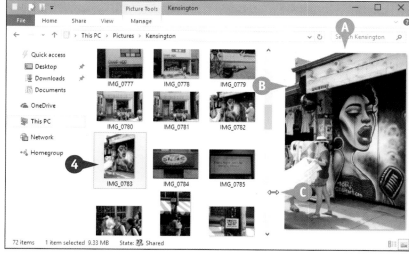

Copy a File

You can use Windows to make an exact copy of a file. This is useful if you want to back up an important file by making an extra copy on a flash drive, memory card, or other removable disc. Similarly, you might require a copy of a file if you want to send the copy on a disc to another person. This section shows you how to copy a single file, but the steps also work if you select multiple files. You can also use these steps to copy a folder.

Copy a File

1 In File Explorer, open the folder containing the file you want to copy.

2 Select the file.

3 Click the **Home** tab.

4 Click **Copy**.

Windows places a copy of the file in a special memory location called the *Clipboard*.

5 Open the location you want to use to store the copy.

6 Click the **Home** tab.

7 Click **Paste**.

Ⓐ Windows inserts a copy of the file in the location.

Move a File

When you need to store a file in a new location, the easiest way is to move the file from its current folder to another folder on your computer. When you save a file for the first time, you specify a folder on your PC's hard drive. This original location is not permanent; you can move the file to another location on the hard drive. This section shows you how to move a single file, but the steps also work if you select multiple files or move a folder.

Move a File

1 In File Explorer, open the folder containing the file you want to move.

2 Select the file.

3 Click the **Home** tab.

4 Click **Cut**.

Windows places the file in the Clipboard.

5 Open the folder to which you want to move the file.

6 Click the **Home** tab.

7 Click **Paste**.

Ⓐ Windows moves the file to the new location.

Rename a File

You can change the name of a file, which is useful if the current name of the file does not accurately describe the file's contents. By giving your document a descriptive name, you make it easier to find the file later.

Make sure that you rename only those documents that you have created or that someone else has given to you. Do not rename any of the Windows system files or any files associated with your programs, or your computer may behave erratically, or even crash.

Rename a File

1 In File Explorer, open the folder that contains the file you want to rename.

2 Click the file.

3 Click the **Home** tab.

Note: In addition to renaming files, you can also rename any folders that you have created.

4 Click **Rename** (or press F2).

A text box appears around the filename.

5 Type the new name you want to use for the file.

Note: If you decide that you do not want to rename the file after all, press Esc to cancel the operation.

Note: The name you type can be up to 255 characters long, but it cannot include the following characters: < > , ? : " \ *.

6 Press Enter or click an empty section of the folder.

The new name appears under the file's icon.

Create a New File

You can quickly create a new file directly within a file folder. This method is faster, and often more convenient, than running a program's New command. In Windows, you can create several different file types, such as a Bitmap Image (a drawing), Rich Text Document (a WordPad file), Text Document (a Notepad file), and Compressed (Zipped) Folder (which combines multiple files in a single file, as described in the section "Extract Files from a Compressed Folder," later in this chapter). You can also create a new folder.

Create a New File

1 In File Explorer, open the folder in which you want to create the file.

2 Click the **Home** tab.

3 Click **New item**.

4 Click the type of file you want to create.

Ⓐ If you click **Folder**, Windows creates a new subfolder.

Note: The New Item menu on your system may contain more items than you see here because some programs install their own file types.

Ⓑ An icon for the new file appears in the folder.

5 Type the name you want to use for the new file.

6 Press Enter.

Delete a File

When you have a file that you no longer need, instead of leaving the file to clutter your hard drive, you can delete it. Make sure that you delete only those documents that you have created or that someone else has given to you. Do not delete any of the Windows system files or any files associated with your programs, or your computer may behave erratically or crash.

Delete a File

1 In File Explorer, open the folder that contains the file you want to delete.

2 Click the file you want to delete.

Note: If you need to remove more than one file, select all the files you want to delete.

Note: See the section "Select a File," earlier in this chapter, to select multiple files.

3 Click the **Home** tab.

4 Click the top half of **Delete**.

Note: Another way to select the Delete command is to press Delete.

A Windows removes the file from the folder.

Note: Another way to delete a file is to click and drag it to the desktop Recycle Bin icon.

240

Restore a Deleted File

If you delete a file in error, Windows enables you to restore the file by placing it back in the folder from which you deleted it. You can restore a deleted file because Windows stores each deleted file in a special folder called the Recycle Bin, where the file stays for a few days or a few weeks, depending on how often you empty the bin or how full the folder becomes.

Restore a Deleted File

1 Double-click the desktop **Recycle Bin** icon.

Note: If you have a touch PC, open File Explorer, click the first **>** in the address bar, and then click **Recycle Bin**.

The Recycle Bin folder appears.

2 Click the file you want to restore.

3 Click the **Manage** tab.

4 Click **Restore the selected items**.

The file disappears from the Recycle Bin and reappears in its original folder.

Add a File to Your OneDrive

If you are using Windows under a Microsoft account, then as part of that account you get a free online storage area called *OneDrive*. You can use the special OneDrive folder on your PC to move or copy any of your files to your OneDrive. This is useful if you are going to be away from your computer but still require access to a file. Because the OneDrive is accessible anywhere you have web access, you can view and work with your file without using your computer.

Add a File to Your OneDrive

Move a File to Your OneDrive

1 In File Explorer, open the folder that contains the file you want to move.

2 Click and drag the file to the **OneDrive** folder.

A As you drag, if you hover the file over **OneDrive**, File Explorer expands OneDrive to let you see your other OneDrive folders.

3 Drop the file on the OneDrive folder you want to use.

B File Explorer moves the file to the OneDrive folder.

Copy a File to Your OneDrive

1. In File Explorer, open the folder that contains the file you want to copy.

2. Press and hold **Ctrl** and then click and drag the file to the **OneDrive** folder.

C. If needed, hover the file over **OneDrive** to see your other OneDrive folders.

3. Drop the file on the OneDrive folder you want to use.

D. File Explorer copies the file to the OneDrive folder.

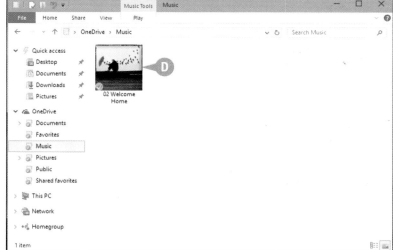

TIPS

How do I access my OneDrive online?

You need to open Microsoft Edge and navigate to the OneDrive site, http://onedrive.live.com. After you are logged in to your OneDrive, you can use it to create new folders, rename files, delete files, and more.

Can I create new documents using OneDrive?

Yes. As part of your OneDrive, Microsoft gives you access to the Office Web Apps, which are scaled-down, online versions of the Microsoft Office applications. To create a document using one of these programs, navigate to your online OneDrive, click **Create**, and then click **Word document**, **Excel workbook**, **PowerPoint presentation**, **OneNote notebook**, **Excel survey**, or **Plain text document**.

Extract Files from a Compressed Folder

I f someone sends you a file via email, or if you download a file from the Internet, the file often arrives in a *compressed* form, which means the file actually contains one or more files that have been compressed to save space. To use the files on your computer, you need to extract them from the compressed file.

Because a compressed file can contain one or more files, it acts like a kind of folder. Therefore, Windows calls such files *compressed folders*, *zipped folders*, or *Zip archives*. You can view these files or extract them from the folder.

Extract Files from a Compressed Folder

View Compressed Folder Files

1 In File Explorer, open the folder containing the compressed folder.

A The compressed folder usually appears as a folder icon with a zipper.

2 Double-click the compressed folder.

B File Explorer displays the contents of the compressed folder.

Note: File Explorer is only displaying the contents of a compressed folder; it has not extracted the files. To extract the files, follow the steps in the next subsection.

Extract Compressed Folder Files

1 In File Explorer, open the folder containing the compressed folder.

2 Click the compressed folder.

3 Click the **Extract** tab.

4 Click **Extract all**.

The Select a Destination and Extract Files dialog box of the Extract Wizard appears.

5 Type the location of the folder into which you want to extract the files.

C You can also click **Browse** and choose the folder.

6 If you want to open the folder into which you extracted the files, click **Show extracted files when complete** (□ changes to ✔).

7 Click **Extract**.

Windows extracts the files.

TIP

How can I create a compressed folder?
Follow these steps:

1 Select the files and folders you want to store in the compressed folder.

2 Right-click any selected item.

3 Click **Send to**.

4 Click **Compressed (zipped) folder**.

The compressed folder appears.

Specify a Different Program When Opening a File

You can open a file in a different program from the one normally associated with the file. This enables you to use the other program's features to work on the file.

You may have situations where you prefer to open a particular file with a different program. For example, double-clicking a picture file opens it in the Photos app. However, you may prefer to open the picture file in Paint or some other image-editing program so that you can make changes to the picture. This section shows you how to open any document in another program.

Specify a Different Program When Opening a File

1 In File Explorer, open the folder that contains the file you want to open.

2 Click the file.

3 Click the **Open** ▼.

Ⓐ If the program you want to use appears here, click the program and skip the remaining steps.

4 Click **Choose another app**.

Windows asks how you want to open this file type.

5 Click **More apps**.

B Windows displays a full list of programs you can use to open the file.

6 Click the program you want to use to open the file.

C If the program you want to use does not appear in the list, you can click **Look for another app on this PC** and use the Open With dialog box to specify the program.

7 Click **OK**.

Windows opens the file in the program you chose.

How can I open every file of the same type in the new program?

If you want to open every file of the same type — such as Text Document files or Rich Text Format files — in the same program, follow steps **1** to **6** and then click **Always use this app to open .*ext* files** (☐ changes to ☑).

Can I set the default program for multiple file types?

Yes. In the taskbar's Search box, type **set default**, click **Default Programs**, and then click **Set your default programs**. Click the program you want to use, click **Choose defaults for this program**, click each file type you want to open with the program (☐ changes to ☑), and then click **Save**.

Sharing Your Computer

If you share your computer with other people, you can create separate user accounts so that each person works only with his own documents, programs, and Windows settings. This chapter shows you how to create and change user accounts, how to log on and off different accounts, how to share documents between accounts, and how to connect and work with a homegroup.

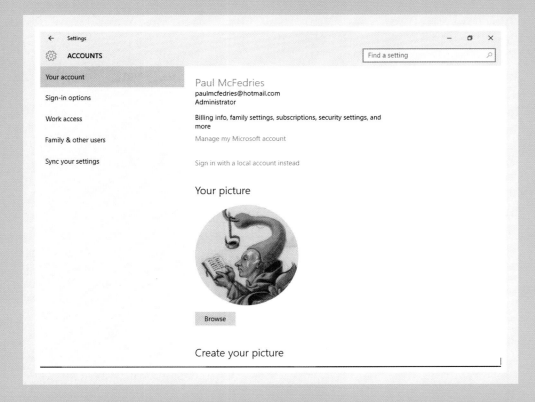

Display User Accounts

To work with user accounts, you need to display the Windows Accounts settings. A *user account* is a collection of Windows folders and settings associated with one person. In this chapter, you learn how to create new user accounts, change a user account's picture, change a user account's password, and delete a user account. To perform any of these tasks, you must first display the Accounts screen of the Settings app.

Display User Accounts

1 Click **Start** (⊞).

The Start menu appears.

2 Click your user account.

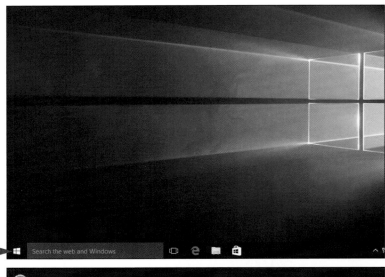

3 Click **Change account settings**.

The Accounts screen appears.

A Information about your account appears here. Later, after you have switched to another account, information for the current account appears in this spot.

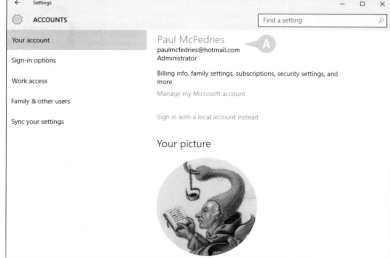

TIP

How do user accounts help me share my computer with other people?

Without other people having their own user accounts, anyone who uses your computer can view and even change your documents, Windows settings, email accounts and messages, Microsoft Edge favorites, and more.

With user accounts for each person, users get their own folders (Documents, Pictures, Music, and so on), personalized Windows settings, email accounts, and favorites. In short, users get their own versions of Windows to personalize without interfering with anyone else's. Also, user accounts enable you to safely share documents and folders with people who use your computer and with people on your network.

Create a User Account

If you want to share your computer with another person, you need to create a user account for that individual. This enables the person to log on to Windows and use the system. The new user account is completely separate from your own account. This means that the other person can change settings, create documents, and perform other Windows tasks without interfering with your settings or data.

You can create a local user account or a Microsoft account. For maximum privacy, you should safeguard each account with a password.

Create a User Account

1 Display the Accounts screen of the Settings app.

Note: See the previous section, "Display User Accounts," to learn how to display the Accounts screen.

2 Click **Family & other users**.

3 Click **Add someone else to this PC**.

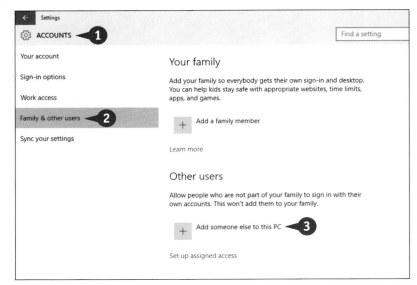

The How Will This Person Sign In screen appears.

4 For a local account, click **The person I want to add doesn't have an email address**.

Note: If you want to create a Microsoft account instead, see Chapter 1 for more information.

5 Click **Add a user without a Microsoft Local account**.

The Create an Account for this PC screen appears.

6 Type the name you want to use for the new account.

7 Type the password.

Note: The password characters appear as dots for security reasons.

8 Type the password again.

9 Type a hint that will help you or the user remember the password.

10 Click **Next**.

Windows creates the account and adds it to the Other Users section.

How do I create a secure password?

It is a good idea to use secure passwords that a nefarious user cannot guess. First, do not use an obvious password such as the user's account name or the word "password." Second, make sure the password is at least eight characters long. Finally, use at least one character from at least three of the following four sets: lowercase letters, uppercase letters, numbers, and symbols.

Switch Between Accounts

After you have created more than one account on your computer, you can switch between accounts. This is useful when one person is already working in Windows and another person needs to use the computer.

When you switch to a second account, Windows leaves the original user's programs and windows running. This means that after the second person is finished, the original user can sign on again and continue working as before.

Switch Between Accounts

1 Click **Start** (⊞).

The Start menu appears.

2 Click your user account.

3 Click the user account you want to switch to.

Windows prompts you for the user account password.

4 Type the password.

5 Click **Submit** ().

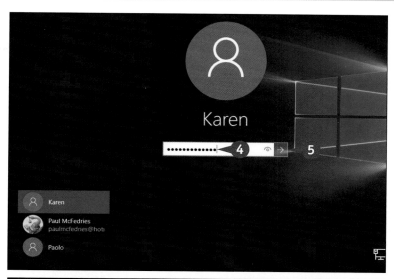

A The user's name and picture now appear in the Start menu.

Note: The first time you switch to a new account, Windows takes a few moments to configure the account.

TIP

What happens if I forget my password?
When you set up your password as described in the previous section, "Create a User Account," Windows asks you to supply a hint to help you remember the password. If you cannot remember your password, follow these steps: In the sign-on screen, leave the password text box blank. Click **Submit** (➡). Windows tells you the password is incorrect. Click **OK** to return to the sign-on screen. Windows displays the password hint.

Change Your User Account Picture

You can add visual interest to your user account as well as make it easier to tell one user account from another by adding a picture to the account. When you create a user account, Windows assigns it a default picture, which appears in the user's Start screen tile, the Accounts screen of the Settings app, and the sign-on screen. Unfortunately, this default picture is a generic silhouette of a person's head and upper torso, so it is not very interesting or useful. If you have a more suitable picture that you would prefer to use, you can change your picture.

Change Your User Account Picture

1 Click **Start** (⊞).

The Start menu appears.

2 Click the user account.

3 Click **Change account settings**.

The Settings app appears with the Your Account tab displayed.

4 Click **Browse**.

The Open dialog box appears.

5 Click the picture you want to use.

6 Click **Choose picture**.

Ⓐ The Your Account tab appears and displays the new picture.

How do I use a webcam photo as my user account picture?
Repeat steps **1** to **3** and then click **Camera** to open the Camera app. Position yourself within the screen and then click the screen to take the picture. The Camera app displays the photo and adds a rectangle that defines the area of the photo it will use for your account picture. Click and drag the rectangle to the position you want. Click and drag the rectangle corners to set the size and shape of the rectangle. Click **OK**.

Change a User's Password

If you set up a user account with no password, or if you find it difficult to remember your password, you can change the password. Assigning a password to each user account is good practice because otherwise someone who sits down at the PC can sign in using an unprotected account.

It is also good practice to assign a strong password to each account, so that a malicious user cannot guess the password and gain access to the system. Whether you want to assign a password or create a password that is stronger or easier to remember, you can use Windows to change an existing password.

Change a User's Password

1 If you want to change another user's password, sign in as that user.

2 Display the Accounts screen of the Settings app.

Note: See the section "Display User Accounts," earlier in this chapter, to learn how to display the Accounts screen.

3 Click **Sign-in options**.

4 Under Password, click **Change**.

Note: If the account has no password, click **Add** in the Password section.

Windows prompts you to verify your current password.

Note: If the account has no current password, skip to step **7**.

5 Type your current account password.

6 Click **Next**.

Windows prompts you for the new password.

7 Type the new password.

8 Type the new password again.

A If you are not sure whether you typed a password correctly, click and hold **Display Password Characters** (👁) to temporarily display the password.

9 Type a hint.

10 Click **Next**.

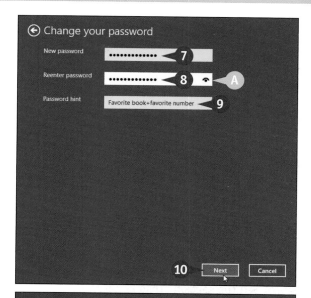

11 Click **Finish**.

Windows updates the user account password.

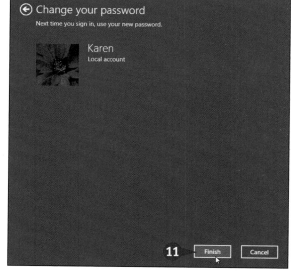

Are there any other precautions I can take to protect my password?
Yes, besides creating a strong password, you can safeguard your password by following these guidelines:

• Do not tell anyone your password.

• Do not write down your password.

• Make your password easier to remember by using a mnemonic device. For example, you could use the first letters as well as any numbers that appear in the name of a favorite book or movie.

Delete an Account

If you create a user account temporarily, or if you have a user account that is no longer needed or no longer used, you can delete that account. This reduces the number of users that appear in the Users tab of the Settings app, as well as the Windows sign-on screen, which can make these screens a bit easier to navigate. Deleting a user account also means that Windows reclaims the hard drive space that the account uses, which gives you more room to store files in your other accounts.

Delete an Account

1 Sign out of the user account you want to delete.

Note: To sign out of an account, click **Start** (⊞), click the user account on the Start menu, and then click **Sign out**.

2 Display the Accounts screen of the Settings app.

Note: See the section "Display User Accounts," earlier in this chapter, to learn how to display the Accounts screen.

3 Click **Family & other users**.

The Family & Other Users screen appears.

4 Click the user account you want to delete.

5 Click **Remove**.

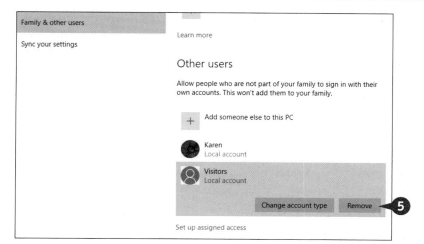

The Delete Account and Data dialog box appears.

6 Click **Delete account and data**.

Windows deletes the account.

Why can I not delete my original Windows account?
Windows configures the original user account as the administrator account on the computer, which means it is the only account allowed to perform tasks such as creating and deleting user accounts. Windows does not allow you to delete this account because it requires that there always be at least one administrator account on the computer. When you are logged in with another account, you cannot access the Other Accounts screen, so you cannot use it to delete your original Windows account.

Create a Homegroup

You can share documents and media easily with other Windows computers by creating a homegroup on your network. A homegroup simplifies network sharing by making it easy to create a homegroup and share documents with other computers and users who are also connected to that homegroup.

You use one Windows computer to create the homegroup, and then you use the homegroup password to join your other Windows computers. For more information, see the next section, "Join a Homegroup."

Create a Homegroup

1. In the taskbar's Search box, type **homegroup**.

2. Click **HomeGroup**.

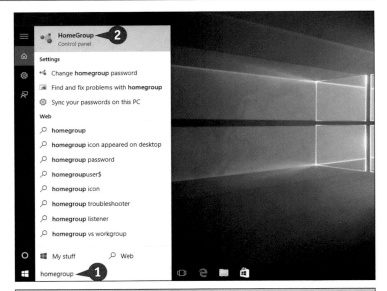

The HomeGroup window appears.

3. Click **Create a homegroup**.

Windows displays an overview of what you can do with a homegroup.

4. Click **Next** (not shown).

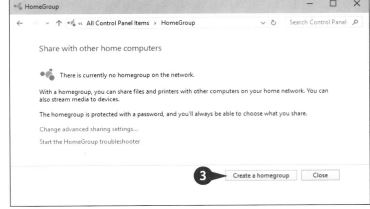

The Create a Homegroup dialog box appears.

5 Select **Shared** for each item you want to share with the homegroup.

6 Click **Next**.

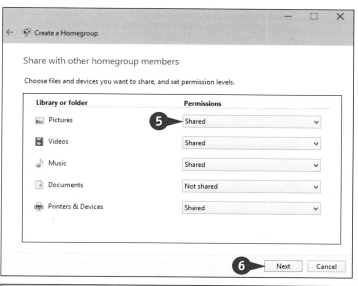

Windows displays the homegroup password.

7 Make a mental note of the homegroup password.

8 Click **Finish**.

You can now join your other computers to the homegroup, as described in the next section. Note that a computer must be running Windows 7 or later to join a homegroup.

I have lost my homegroup password. How do I view it again?
The easiest method is to repeat steps **1** and **2** to display the HomeGroup window and then click **View or print the homegroup password**. The window that appears displays the homegroup password.

How can I change the homegroup password?
Follow steps **1** and **2** to display the HomeGroup window. Click the **Change the password** link and then click **Change the password** to generate a new homegroup password. If one or more computers have already joined the homegroup, you need to provide them with the new password.

Join a Homegroup

If your network has a homegroup, you can join your Windows computer to that homegroup. This enables you to access shared resources on other homegroup computers, and to share your own resources with the homegroup.

This section assumes you or someone else on your home network has already set up a homegroup as described in the previous section, "Create a Homegroup," and that you have the homegroup password.

Join a Homegroup

1 In the taskbar's Search box, type **homegroup**.

2 Click **HomeGroup**.

The HomeGroup window appears.

3 Click **Join now**.

Windows displays an overview of what you can do with a homegroup.

4 Click **Next** (not shown).

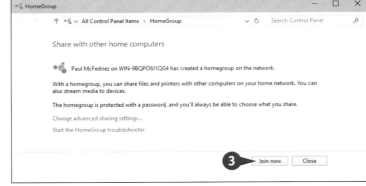

The Share with Other Homegroup Members dialog box appears.

5 Select **Shared** for each item you want to share with the homegroup.

6 Click **Next**.

Windows prompts you for the homegroup password.

7 Type the homegroup password.

8 Click **Next**.

Windows joins the homegroup.

9 Click **Finish**.

You can now access other homegroup computers and share your files with the homegroup.

When I try to join a homegroup, Windows tells me my password is not correct. What am I doing wrong?

First, double-check that you have been given the correct homegroup password and that you are typing that password correctly. Second, understand that homegroup passwords are case-sensitive, so you must type the uppercase and lowercase letters exactly as they appear in the original homegroup settings. Make sure your keyboard does not have Caps Lock turned on.

Can I leave a homegroup if I no longer need it?

Yes. Follow steps **1** and **2** to display the HomeGroup window. Click **Leave the homegroup**. When Windows asks you to confirm, click **Leave the homegroup**.

Share a Document or Folder

You can share documents and folders of your choice with your homegroup, if your network has one. You can also share a document or folder with other users set up on your computer.

Sharing a document or folder enables you to work on a file with other people without having to send them a copy of the file. You can set up each document or folder with View or View and Edit permissions. View permission means that users cannot make changes to the document or folder; View and Edit permission means that users can view and make changes to the document or folder.

Share a Document or Folder

Share with the Homegroup

1. Click **File Explorer** (📁).

2. Open the folder containing the item you want to share.

3. Click the document or folder you want to share.

4. Click the **Share** tab.

5. Click **Homegroup (view)**.

Ⓐ To allow homegroup users to make changes to the item, click **Homegroup (view and edit)** instead.

Share with a Specific User

1. Open the folder containing the item you want to share.

2. Click the document or folder you want to share.

3. Click the **Share** tab.

4. Click **Specific people**.

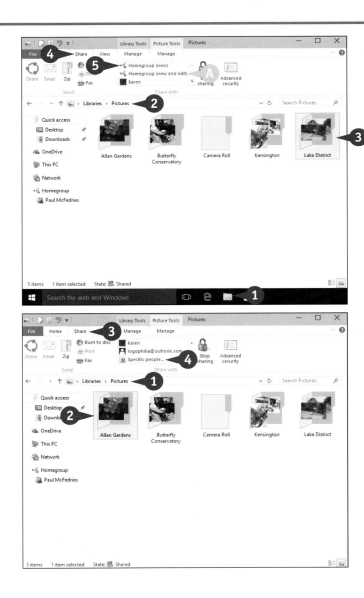

The File Sharing dialog box appears.

5 Click ✓ and then click the name of the user.

6 Click **Add**.

7 Click ▼ and then click the permission level.

Note: Read permission is the same as View, and Read/Write is the same as View and Edit.

8 Click **Share**.

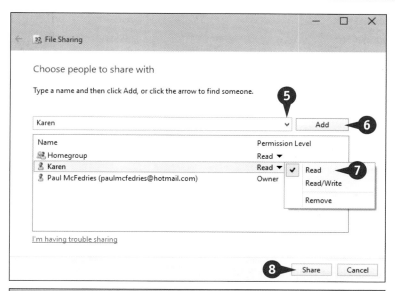

Windows shares the document or folder.

B Be sure to give the user the address that appears here.

9 Click **Done**.

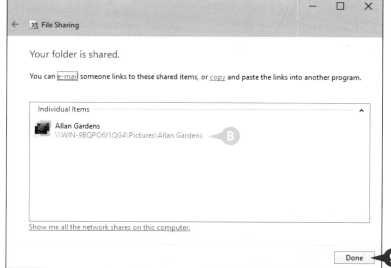

TIPS

How do the other users access the shared document or folder?

Send them the address in the final File Sharing dialog box. You have two choices: Click **e-mail** to send the address via email, or click **copy** to copy the address to memory. You can then open a program such as WordPad, click **Edit**, and then click **Paste** to paste the address.

Can I see all the documents and folders that I am sharing with other users?

Yes, you can do this in two ways. In the final File Sharing dialog box, click **Show me all the network shares on this computer**. Alternatively, in any folder window, click **Network** and then double-click your computer.

View Network Resources

To see what other network users have shared in your homegroup, you can use the Homegroup folder to view the other computers and see their shared resources. To get access to the shared homegroup resources, you must know the homegroup's password and have joined the homegroup, as described earlier in the section "Join a Homegroup." If your network does not have a homegroup, you can use the Network folder instead. A network resource can be a folder, hard drive, CD or DVD drive, flash drive, printer, scanner, or other shared device.

View Network Resources

View Homegroup Resources

1 Click **File Explorer** (▢).

2 Click the **Homegroup** folder.

Ⓐ Windows displays icons for each user who is sharing data in the homegroup.

3 Double-click the user who is sharing the resource you want to access.

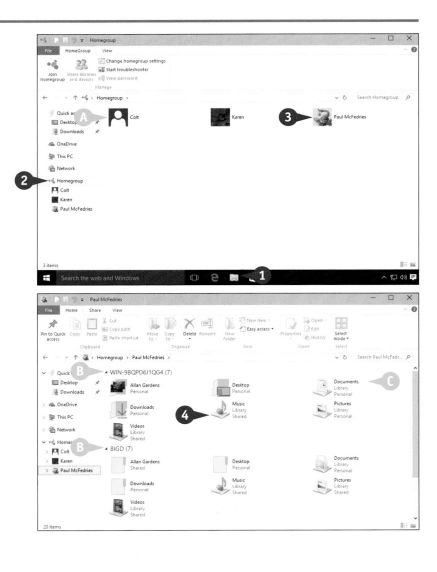

Windows displays the resources the user is sharing.

Ⓑ If the user has an account on multiple PCs, you see a section for each PC.

Ⓒ The resources that the user is sharing on the computer appear here.

4 Double-click an icon to access the resource.

View Network Resources

1 In File Explorer, click the **Network** folder.

D Windows displays icons for each computer that is sharing resources.

2 Double-click the computer that is sharing the resource you want to access.

E The resources the computer is sharing appear here.

3 Double-click an icon to access the resource.

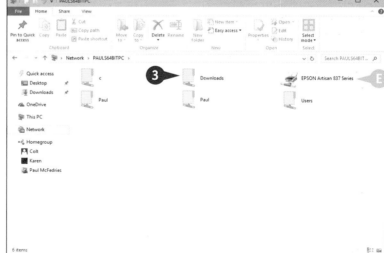

TIPS

How can I fix network problems?
If you are having homegroup trouble, launch File Explorer, click the **Homegroup** folder, click the **Homegroup** tab, and then click **Start troubleshooter**. If you are having network trouble, right-click the network icon in the taskbar's notification area and then click **Troubleshoot problems**. In both cases, follow whatever repair techniques Windows suggests.

How do I change my computer's network name?
In the taskbar's Search box, type **name** and then click **View your PC name**. Windows opens the PC screen of the Settings app. Click **Rename PC**, use the Rename Your PC text box to type the new name, click **Next**, and then click **Restart now**.

Getting More from a Tablet PC

Windows comes with many features designed to help you get the most out of your tablet PC. In this chapter, you learn how to use gestures, type with and configure the touch keyboard, add a second monitor, and more.

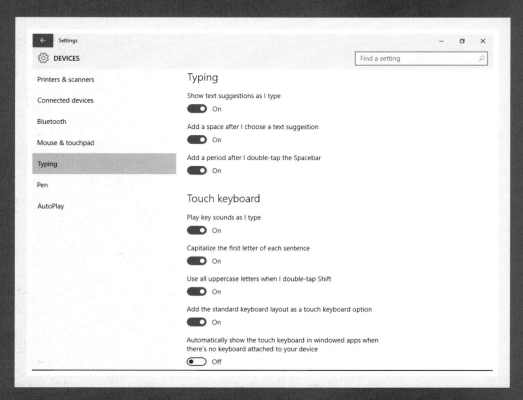

Shut Down an App

1 Place your finger or stylus at the top edge of the app screen.

2 Slide down until the app window turns into a thumbnail, and then slide the thumbnail down to the bottom of the screen.

Windows shuts down the app.

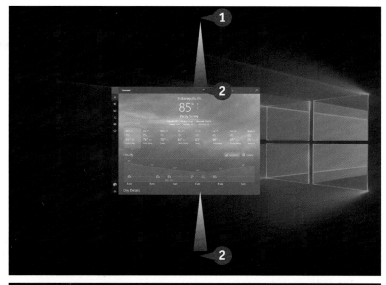

Move an Item

1 Position your finger or the stylus over the item that you want to move.

2 Tap and hold the item and immediately begin moving your finger or the stylus.

E The object moves along with your finger or the stylus.

3 When the object is repositioned where you want it, lift your finger or the stylus off the screen to complete the move.

TIP

How do I use gestures to select files and folders in File Explorer?
You can use the following techniques:

- To select a single file or folder, tap it.
- To select multiple, adjacent files or folders, tap and hold the screen above and to the left of the first item, and then slide your finger or stylus down and to the right until you have selected the items you want.
- If you have a physical keyboard, you can select multiple, nonadjacent files or folders by tapping the first one, pressing and holding Shift, and then tapping the other items you want to select.

Input Text with the Touch Keyboard

If you are using a tablet, or a PC in tablet mode, you do not have a physical keyboard available. To input text, Windows offers the *touch keyboard*, which is a virtual keyboard that appears on the screen. You input text using this keyboard by tapping the keys. Windows offers several touch keyboard types, and some characters are difficult to find, so you need to know how to use the touch keyboard to get the most out of Windows.

Input Text with the Touch Keyboard

Select a Keyboard

1 In an app, tap the text box area in which you want to insert text.

A Windows displays the touch keyboard.

2 Tap **Keyboard** (⌨).

Windows displays the keyboard options.

B You can tap ⌨ for the default keyboard.

C You can tap ⌨ for the split keyboard.

D You can tap ✐ for the writing pad.

Input Text

1 Tap the keys for the characters that you want to input.

Windows inserts the text.

E To enter an uppercase letter, you can tap **Shift** (⬆) and then tap the letter.

F To delete the previous character, you can tap **Backspace** (⌫).

2 To enter numbers and other symbols, tap &123.

Windows displays the numbers and symbols.

③ Tap **More** (⊙) to see more symbols.

④ To see more symbols, tap and hold a key.

Ⓖ Windows displays the extra symbols.

⑤ Slide your finger to the symbol that you want and then release.

Ⓗ You can tap **Back** (⊙) to return to the previous symbols.

Ⓘ You can tap &123 to return to the letters.

⑥ When you are done, tap **Close** (⊠) to hide the keyboard.

TIP

How do I write text with the stylus?
Follow steps **1** and **2** in the subsection "Select a Keyboard" and then tap **Writing Pad** (✍). Use the stylus to handwrite the text in the writing pad (Ⓐ). As you write, Windows converts your writing to text and adds it to the text box. To insert a space, tap **Space** (⎵) (Ⓑ).

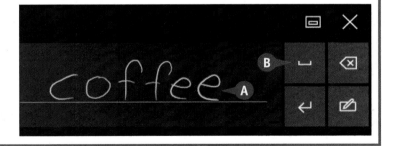

Configure the Touch Keyboard

The touch keyboard offers a number of features that make it easier to use. For example, the touch keyboard automatically adds a period and space when you double-tap the spacebar, and it automatically capitalizes the first letter of each sentence.

However, the touch keyboard also has some features that you might not like — such as the noise it makes each time you tap a key. You can use the Settings app to turn on the touch keyboard features that you like and turn off the features that you do not like.

Configure the Touch Keyboard

1 Tap **Start** (▦).

2 Tap **Menu** (≡).

The Start menu appears.

3 Tap **Settings**.

The Settings app appears.

④ Tap **Devices**.

The Devices screen appears.

⑤ Tap **Typing**.

⑥ Under Touch Keyboard, tap each option **On** or **Off**, according to your preferences.

Windows applies your new settings to the touch keyboard.

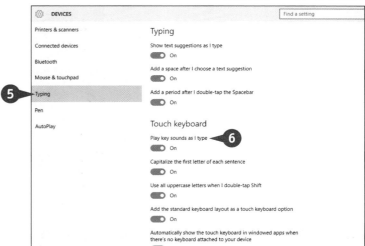

TIP

What is the standard keyboard layout?
If you tap the **Add the standard keyboard layout as a touch keyboard option** switch to **On** in step **6**, the next time that you use the keyboard, tap ⌨ and then tap ⌨. This presents a keyboard with all the keys on a normal keyboard.

Configure Your Tablet to Work with a Second Monitor

You can improve your productivity and efficiency by using a second monitor. To work with an external monitor, your tablet must have a video output port, such as VGA, DVI, or HDMI. If you do not have such a port, check with the manufacturer to see if an adapter is available that enables your tablet to connect with an external monitor.

After you have connected your tablet and the external monitor, you then need to configure Windows to extend the Start screen to both the tablet screen and the external monitor.

Configure Your Tablet to Work with a Second Monitor

1. Connect the second monitor to your tablet.

2. Tap **Start** (⊞).

3. Tap **Menu** (≡).

4. Tap **Settings**.

The Settings app appears.

5. Tap **System**.

The System screen appears.

6 Tap **Display**.

7 Tap the **Multiple displays** ∨ and then tap **Extend these displays**.

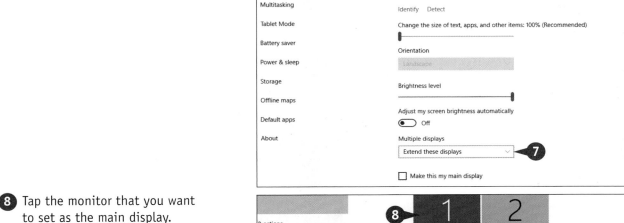

8 Tap the monitor that you want to set as the main display.

9 Tap **Make this my main display** (☐ changes to ☑).

10 Tap **Apply**.

Windows connects to the second monitor, uses it to extend the desktop, and uses the monitor that you selected as your main display.

TIP

Why does my cursor stop at the right edge of the left screen?
Ideally, you should be able to move your cursor continuously from the left monitor to the right monitor. If you find that the cursor stops at the right edge of your left monitor, it means that you need to exchange the icons of the left and right monitors. To do that, follow steps **1** to **6**, and then tap and drag the left monitor icon to the right of the other monitor icon (or vice versa).

Adjust Screen Brightness

You can extend the battery life of your tablet by turning down the screen brightness. Your tablet screen uses a lot of power, so turning down the brightness also reduces battery drain.

On the other hand, if you have trouble seeing the data on your tablet screen, you can often fix the problem by *increasing* the screen brightness. This is not a problem when your tablet is running on AC power. However, you should not use full screen brightness for very long when your tablet is running on its battery because a bright screen uses a lot of power.

Adjust Screen Brightness

1 Tap **Power** (▢).

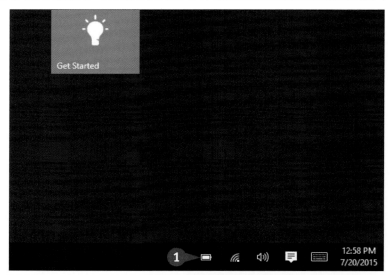

The Power options appear.

2 Tap the brightness setting to cycle through one of four screen brightness values: 25%, 50%, 75%, and 100%.

Windows puts the new brightness setting into effect.

Monitor Battery Life

You can use the Power icon in the Desktop taskbar's notification area to monitor your tablet's remaining battery power. When the battery is at maximum charge, the icon shows as all white. As the battery charge falls, the amount of white in the icon also falls. You can also position your stylus cursor over the icon or tap the icon to see a tool tip that shows you the current battery level.

Monitor Battery Life

1 Tap **Power** (⬚).

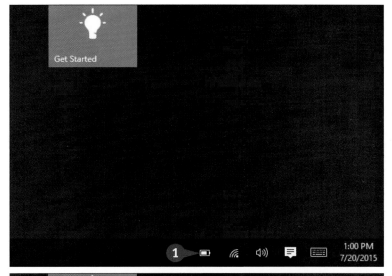

Ⓐ The current battery level appears here.

Implementing Security

Threats to your computing-related security and privacy often come from the Internet and from someone simply using your computer while you are not around. To protect yourself and your family, you need to understand these threats and know what you can do to thwart them.

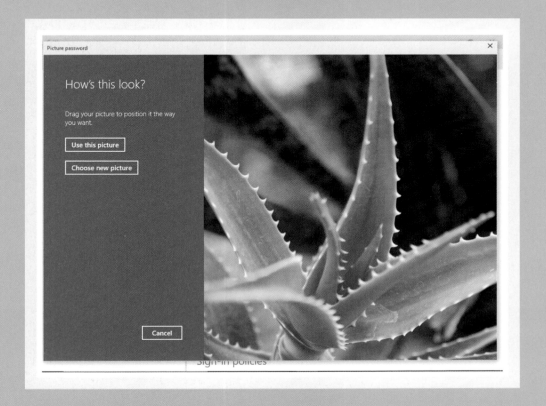

Understanding Windows Security

Before you get to the details of securing your computer, it helps to take a step back and look at the security and privacy tools that Windows makes available.

These tools include your Windows user account password, User Account Control, locking your PC, Windows Firewall, Windows Defender, and the private browsing feature in Microsoft Edge. Taken all together, these features represent a *defense-in-depth* security strategy that uses multiple layers to keep you and your data safe and private.

User Account Password

Windows security begins with assigning a password to each user account on the computer. This prevents unauthorized users from accessing the system, and it enables you to lock your computer. For more information, see the section "Lock Your Computer," later in this chapter.

User Account Control

User Account Control asks you to confirm certain actions that could conceivably harm your system. When you are using your main Windows user account, which is your computer's administrative account, you click **Yes** to continue; for all other accounts, you must enter the administrative account's username and password to continue.

Locking Your PC

Protecting your PC with a password prevents unauthorized access, but what happens when you leave your desk? If you remain logged on, a person who sits down at your computer can view and work with your files. Instead of shutting down your computer when you leave your desk, you can lock your system instead. Anyone who tries to use your computer must first enter your password.

Windows Firewall

When your computer is connected to the Internet, it is possible for another person to access your computer and infect it with a virus or cause other damage; as a result, Windows comes with its Windows Firewall feature turned on. This prevents intruders from accessing your computer while you are online.

Help protect your PC with Windows Firewall

Windows Firewall can help prevent hackers or malicious soft through the Internet or a network.

 Private networks

Networks at home or work where you know and trust the p

Windows Firewall state: On

Windows Defender

Spyware is a software program that installs itself on your computer without your knowledge or consent. This type of program surreptitiously gathers data from your computer, steals your passwords, displays advertisements, and hijacks your web browser. To prevent spyware from installing on your computer, Windows includes the Windows Defender program.

Malware Detected
Windows Defender is taking action to clean detected malware

InPrivate Web Browsing

The Microsoft Edge Explorer web browser normally collects data as you navigate from site to site. Most of this data is used to improve your browsing experience, but it can also be used to track your online activities. If you plan on visiting private or sensitive sites, you can turn on InPrivate browsing, which tells Microsoft Edge not to collect any data during your browsing session. For more information, see the section "Browse the Web Privately," later in this chapter.

Browsing InPrivate

🔍 Search Bing or enter web address →

When you use InPrivate tabs, your browsing data (like cookies, history, or temporary files) isn't saved on your PC after you're done. Microsoft Edge deletes temporary data from your PC after all of your InPrivate tabs are closed.
Read the Microsoft privacy statement

Reset Your PC

Your computer contains a lot of information about you, including your personal files, your Microsoft Edge favorites, your email messages, and your Windows settings. If you plan on selling or donating your computer, you can use the Reset Your PC feature to securely remove your data while installing a fresh copy of Windows.

Reset this PC

If your PC isn't running well, resetting it might help. This lets you choose to keep your files or remove them, and then reinstalls Windows.

Get started

Check for Security Problems

In Windows, the Security and Maintenance window displays messages about the current state of your computer. In particular, it warns you if your computer has any current security problems. For example, Security and Maintenance tells you if your computer does not have virus protection installed or if the Windows Defender spyware database is out of date. Security and Maintenance will also warn you if your computer is not set up to download updates automatically and if important security features such as User Account Control are turned off.

Check for Security Problems

1. In the taskbar's Search box, type **security**.

2. Click **Check security status**.

The Security and Maintenance window appears.

3. Review the messages in the Security section.

4. Click a message button to resolve the security issue, such as clicking **Turn on now** if Windows Defender is turned off.

5 Click **Security**.

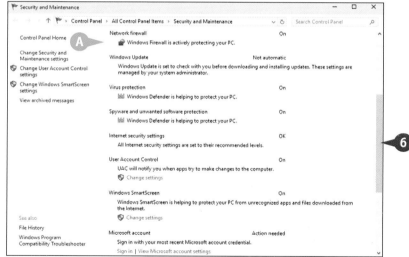

6 Scroll down the Security and Maintenance window.

A Security and Maintenance displays a summary of all your system's security settings.

TIPS

Can I control which messages I see in Security and Maintenance?

Yes. Follow steps **1** and **2** to open the Security and Maintenance window, and then click **Change Security and Maintenance settings**. Click any security or maintenance message you no longer want to see (☑ changes to ☐). Click **OK**.

Do I always have to open the Security and Maintenance window to resolve security issues?

No. In many cases, you can resolve the issue directly without opening Security and Maintenance. In the taskbar's notification area, click **Action Center** (🖥) and examine the window that appears. If you see a security issue, it should also display a link that you can click to resolve the issue.

Create a Picture Password

You can make it easier to sign in to your Windows computer by creating a picture password. This is particularly true for a tablet PC. If you find that it is taking you a long time to sign in to Windows using your tablet's touch keyboard, you can switch to a picture password instead. In this case, your "password" is a series of three gestures — any combination of a click, a straight line, or a circle — that you apply to a photo. Windows displays the photo at startup, and you repeat your gestures, in order, to sign in.

Create a Picture Password

1 In the taskbar's Search box, type **password**.

2 Click **Set up picture password**.

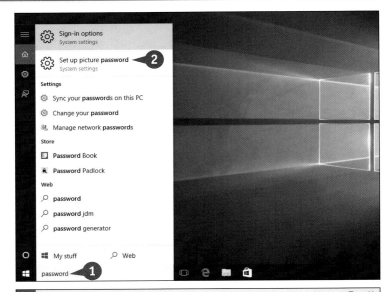

The Settings app appears and displays the Sign-in Options screen.

3 Under Picture Password, click **Add**.

Windows prompts you for your account password.

4 Type your password.

5 Click **OK**.

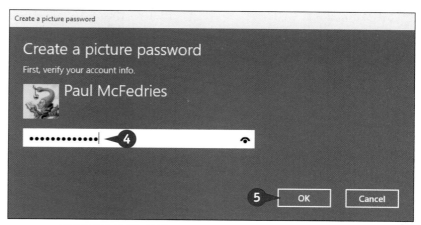

The Welcome to Picture Password screen appears.

6 Click **Choose picture**.

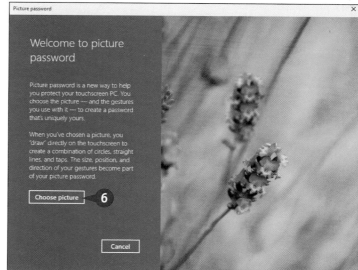

TIPS

Is a picture password safe to use?
Yes. The biggest drawback is that it is possible for a malicious user to view and possibly even record your gestures using a camera. Unlike a regular text password for which the characters appear as dots to prevent someone from seeing them, gestures have no such protection.

Does the picture password replace my text password?
No. Your picture password is applied to your user account along with your existing text-based password. As you see in the next Tips section, it is not difficult to bypass the picture password and sign in using the text password, so you should still protect your PC with a strong text password.

continued ▶

In the same way that you should not choose a regular account password that is extremely obvious, such as the word *password* or your username, you should take care to avoid creating an obvious picture password. For example, if you are using a photo showing three faces, an obvious picture password would be a click on each face.

A good picture password not only uses all three available gestures, but also uses them in nonobvious ways. To ensure that you have memorized your picture password, you should sign out of your account a few times and then sign back on using the picture password.

Create a Picture Password (continued)

The Pictures screen appears.

⑦ Click the picture that you want to use.

⑧ Click **Open**.

The How's This Look screen appears.

⑨ Drag the picture so that the image is positioned where you want.

⑩ Click **Use this picture**.

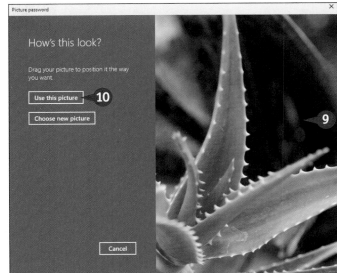

The Set Up Your Gestures screen appears.

11 Use your finger or a stylus to draw three gestures.

12 Repeat the gestures to confirm.

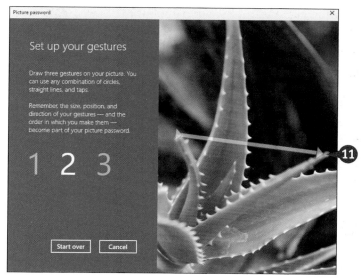

13 Click **Finish**.

The next time that you sign in to Windows, you will be prompted to enter your picture password gestures.

TIPS

What happens if I forget my gestures?

At the sign-on screen, click **Sign-in options** and then click **Microsoft account** to sign in with your regular password. To get a reminder of your picture password gestures, follow steps **1** and **2** in this section, click **Change**, type your user account password, and click **OK**. In the Change Your Picture Password screen, click **Replay**. Click the picture to see each gesture.

Can I change my picture password?

Yes. Open the Change Your Picture Password screen as described in the preceding Tip, choose a new picture, if necessary, and then run through your gestures.

Set Up a Fingerprint Sign-In

You can ensure that only you can access your PC and you can avoid the insecurity of using passwords and gestures in public, by using your fingerprint to sign in to Windows.

If your PC comes with a built-in fingerprint reader, or you have an external reader attached to your PC, you can use the Windows Hello feature to teach Windows your fingerprint and use it to sign in. Because your fingerprint is unique, this ensures that only you can access your PC. Also, if you are in a public place, you do not have to enter a password or use sign-in gestures that could be observed by a nearby snoop.

Set Up a Fingerprint Sign-In

1 In the taskbar's Search box, type **fingerprint**.

2 Click **Set up fingerprint sign-in**.

The Settings app appears and displays the Sign-in Options screen.

3 Under Fingerprint, click **Set up**.

Note: If the Set Up button is disabled, you must assign a PIN to your Microsoft account. In the Sign-in Options screen, click **Add** under the PIN heading and following the prompts to assign a PIN to your account.

The Windows Hello Setup dialog box appears.

4 Click **Get started**.

Windows prompts you for your account PIN.

5 Type your PIN.

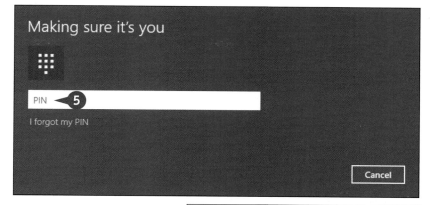

Windows Hello prompts you to scan your fingerprint.

6 Swipe your finger across your PC's fingerprint reader.

7 Repeat the swipe until the scan is complete.

8 Click **Close**.

The next time that you start your PC, you will be prompted to swipe your finger across the fingerprint reader to sign in.

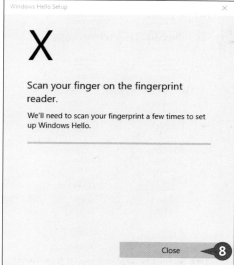

TIPS

What do I do if Windows does not recognize my fingerprint swipe when I try to sign in?

At the sign-on screen, click **Sign-in options** and then click **Microsoft account** to sign in with your regular password.

How do I stop using my fingerprint for signing in to Windows?

To remove your fingerprint from the sign-in options, follow steps **1** and **2** in this section to display the Settings app's Sign-in Options window. Under the Fingerprint section, click **Remove**.

Lock Your Computer

You can enhance your computer's security by locking the device when you leave it unattended. Protecting your account with a password prevents someone from logging on to your account, but what happens when you leave your computer unattended? If you remain logged on to the system, any person who picks up your computer can use it to view and change files.

To prevent this, you can lock your computer. After your computer is locked, anyone who tries to use your computer will first have to enter your password.

Lock Your Computer

Lock Your Computer

1 Click **Start** (⊞).

2 Click your user account.

3 Click **Lock**.

Windows locks your computer and displays the Lock screen.

Unlock Your Computer

1 On the Lock screen, press **Enter** to display the sign-in screen.

2 Click inside the Password text box.

3 Type your password.

4 Click **Submit** (→).

Windows unlocks your computer and restores your desktop.

How can I quickly access the Lock command?

If you need to leave your desk in a hurry, Windows offers a couple of quick methods for locking your computer. Probably the quickest way to lock your computer is to press ⊞+**L**. Alternatively, press **Ctrl**+**Alt**+**Delete** and then click **Lock**.

Configure Your PC to Lock Automatically

You can configure Windows to automatically lock your computer after it has been idle for a specified time.

The previous section describes how to lock your computer to prevent unauthorized access when you leave your PC. However, the hard part is *remembering* to do it. If you are late for a meeting or other appointment, locking your machine is probably the last thing on your mind as you dash out the door. To ensure that some snoop cannot access your PC if you forget to lock it, you can configure Windows to lock automatically after a period of inactivity.

Configure Your PC to Lock Automatically

1 In the taskbar's Search box, type **screen saver**.

2 Click **Change screen saver**.

The Screen Saver Settings dialog box appears.

3 Click **On resume, display logon screen** (☐ changes to ☑).

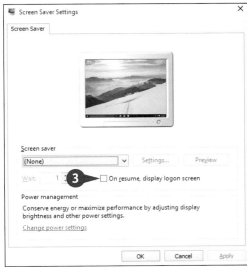

4 Use the **Wait** ⬍ to set the number of minutes of idle that must pass before Windows locks your computer.

5 Click **OK**.

Windows now automatically locks your PC when it has been idle for the number of minutes you specified in step **4**.

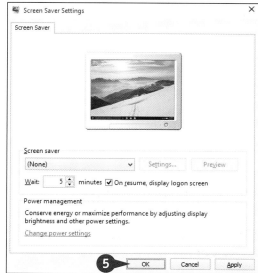

TIP

Does my computer lock when it goes into sleep mode?
Yes, Windows is also configured by default to display the logon screen when your computer wakes up from sleep mode. To make sure this setting is activated, click **Start** (⊞) and then click **Settings** to launch the Settings app. Click **Accounts** to open the Accounts window and then click the **Sign-in options** tab. Click the **Require sign-in** ⌄ and then click **When PC wakes up from sleep**.

Browse the Web Privately

If you visit sensitive or private websites, you can tell Microsoft Edge not to save any browsing history for those sites. If you regularly visit private websites or websites that contain sensitive or secret data, you can ensure that no one else sees any data for such sites by deleting your browsing history, as described in the Tip section. However, if you visit such sites only occasionally, deleting your entire browsing history is overkill. A better solution is to turn on the InPrivate browsing feature in Microsoft Edge before you visit private sites. This tells Microsoft Edge to temporarily stop saving any browsing history.

Browse the Web Privately

1 In the taskbar's Search box, type **edge**.

2 Click **Microsoft Edge**.

Ⓐ Alternatively, you can click **Microsoft Edge** (**e**) if you see it in the taskbar.

3 Click **More** (⋯).

4 Click **New InPrivate window**.

You can also activate InPrivate by pressing `Ctrl` + `Shift` + `P`.

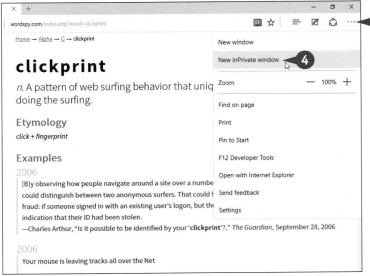

A new Microsoft Edge window appears.

Ⓑ The InPrivate indicator appears in the upper-left corner of the window.

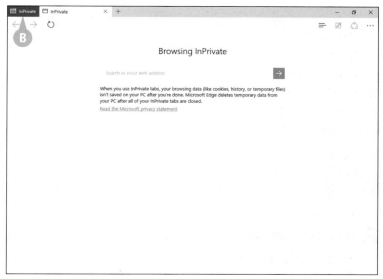

⑤ Surf to and interact with websites as you normally would, such as the banking site shown here.

⑥ When you are done, click **Close** (✕).

Microsoft Edge closes the InPrivate window and turns off InPrivate browsing.

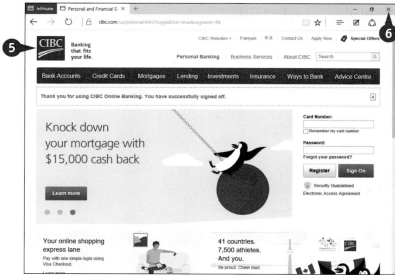

TIP

What is browsing history?

Microsoft Edge maintains a list of the sites that you visit, as well as text and passwords that you have typed into forms, the names of files that you have downloaded, and *cookies*, which are small text files that store information such as site preferences and site logon data. Saving this history is dangerous because other people who use your computer can just as easily visit or view information about those sites. You eliminate this risk by visiting such sites using an InPrivate browsing session. To delete your browsing history, click **More** (···), click **Settings**, click **Choose what to clear**, click **Browsing history** (☐ changes to ☑), and then click **Clear**.

Control Your Private Information

By default, Windows enables apps to access many aspects of your system, such as the camera, microphone, and internal antennas such as Wi-Fi and Bluetooth. Windows also enables apps to access personal information such as your location, account information, contacts, and calendar. This access improves your app experience in most cases, but you might be uncomfortable sharing so much with apps, particularly third-party apps. In that case, you can turn off access to your system resources and to your private information, either globally or just for specific apps.

Control Your Private Information

1 Click **Start** (▦).

2 Click **Settings**.

The Settings app appears.

3 Click **Privacy**.

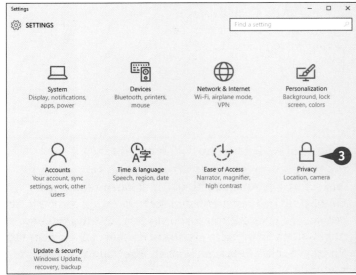

The Privacy screen appears.

④ Click **Location**.

⑤ Click the **Location** switch to **Off** to prevent apps from using your location.

⑥ To remove all location information from your PC, click **Clear**.

Windows removes all your location information.

⑦ For each resource that you no longer want to allow apps to access, click the resource tab.

⑧ Click the switch that controls global access to **Off**.

Ⓐ Alternatively, you can use the app-specific switches to turn off access for individual apps.

The next time you display the Start menu, you will not see any personal information in the tiles.

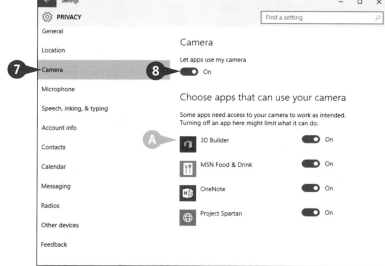

How do I prevent Windows from showing apps and documents that I have used recently?
Click **Start** (⊞), click **Settings**, click **Personalization**, and then click **Start**. To prevent Windows from showing recent apps and documents, click the **Store and display recently opened programs in Start** switch to **Off** and then click the **Store and display recently opened items in Start and the taskbar** switch to **Off**.

How do I stop an app's notifications?
If an app's notifications contain private information, you can turn them off. Click **Start** (⊞), click **Settings**, click **System**, and then click **Notifications & actions**. Beside the app for which you want notifications disabled, click the switch to **Off**.

Reset Your Computer to Preserve Privacy

As you use your computer, you accumulate a large amount of personal data: documents, installed apps, Microsoft Edge favorites, email messages, photos, and much more. If you are selling your computer or giving it away, you probably do not want the recipient to have access to all that personal data. To prevent this, you can reset the computer, which deletes all your personal data and reinstalls a fresh copy of Windows.

Reset Your Computer to Preserve Privacy

Note: This section assumes that you have copied your personal files to a backup destination, such as an external hard drive.

1. In the taskbar's Search box, type **reset.**

2. Click **Reset this PC.**

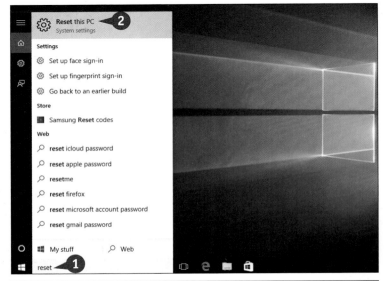

The Settings app opens and displays the Update & Security window.

3. Under Reset this PC, click **Get started**.

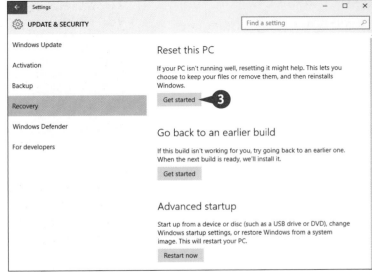

Windows asks how you want to remove your personal files.

4 Click the removal option that you want.

Note: For more information about the removal options, see the Tip.

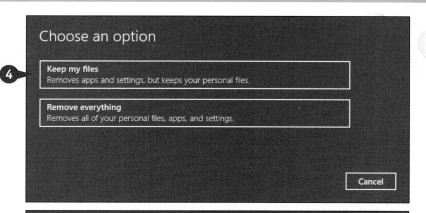

Windows displays a list of apps that will be removed during the reset process.

5 Click **Next**.

The Ready to Reset This PC screen appears.

6 Click **Reset**.

Windows resets your computer.

TIP

What is the difference between removing my files and fully cleaning the drive?
The Keep My Files option deletes your apps and your Windows settings, but it leaves your files on your PC, so this is not the option you want if you are giving away or selling your PC. Instead, you want the Remove Everything option, which not only removes your apps and your custom Windows settings, but it also removes all your personal files.

Maintaining Windows

To keep your system running smoothly, maintain top performance, and reduce the risk of computer problems, you need to perform some routine maintenance chores. This chapter shows you how to delete unnecessary files, check for hard drive and other device errors, back up your files, and more.

Check Hard Drive Free Space

To ensure that your PC's hard drive does not become full, you should periodically check how much free space it has left. This is important because if you run out of room on your hard drive, you cannot install more programs or create more documents, and your PC's performance will suffer.

Of particular concern is the hard drive on which Windows is installed, usually drive C. If this hard drive's free space becomes low — say, less than about 20 or 25GB — Windows runs slowly. With normal computer use, you should check your hard drive free space about once a month.

Check Hard Drive Free Space

Note: You can also check the free space on a CD, DVD, memory card, or flash drive. Before you continue, insert the disc, card, or drive.

1 Click **File Explorer**.

File Explorer appears.

2 Click **This PC**.

The This PC folder appears.

3 Click the **View** tab.

4 Click **Tiles**.

Ⓐ Information about each drive appears along with the drive icon.

Ⓑ This value tells you the amount of free space on the drive.

Ⓒ This value tells you the total amount of space on the drive.

Ⓓ This bar gives you a visual indication of how much disk space the drive is using.

Ⓔ Windows is installed on the drive with the Windows logo (🪟).

Ⓕ The used portion of the bar appears blue when a drive still has sufficient disk space.

Ⓖ The used portion of the bar turns red when a drive's disk space becomes low.

⑤ Click **Close** (✕) to close the This PC window.

What can I do if my hard drive space is becoming low?

You can do three things:

- **Delete Personal Files**. If you have personal files — particularly media files such as images, music, and videos — that you no longer need, delete them.
- **Remove Programs**. If you have programs that you no longer use, uninstall them (see Chapter 1).
- **Run Disk Cleanup**. Use the Disk Cleanup program to delete files that Windows no longer uses. See the next section, "Delete Unnecessary Files."

Delete Unnecessary Files

To free up hard drive space on your computer and keep Windows running efficiently, you can use the Disk Cleanup program to delete files that your system no longer needs. Although today's hard drives are quite large, it is still possible to run low on disk space, particularly because today's applications and media files are larger than ever.

Run Disk Cleanup any time that your hard drive free space becomes too low. If hard drive space is not a problem, run Disk Cleanup every two or three months.

Delete Unnecessary Files

1 Click **File Explorer**.

File Explorer appears.

2 Click **This PC**.

The This PC folder appears.

3 Click the hard drive you want to clean.

4 Click the **Manage** tab.

5 Click **Cleanup**.

After a few moments, the Disk Cleanup dialog box appears.

A This area displays the total amount of drive space you can free up.

B This area displays the amount of drive space the activated options will free up.

6 Click the check box (☐ changes to ☑) for each file type that you want to delete.

C This area displays a description of the highlighted file type.

7 Click **OK**.

Disk Cleanup asks you to confirm that you want to delete the file types.

8 Click **Delete Files**.

TIP

What types of files does Disk Cleanup delete?
It deletes the following file types:

- **Downloaded Program Files**. These are small web page programs downloaded onto your hard drive.
- **Temporary Internet Files**. These are web page copies stored on your hard drive for faster viewing.
- **Delivery Optimization Files**. These are files used by Windows' Delivery Optimization service.
- **Recycle Bin**. These are files that you have deleted since you last emptied your Recycle Bin.
- **Temporary Files**. These are files used by programs to store temporary data.
- **Thumbnails**. These are miniature versions of images and other content used in folder windows.

Refresh Your Computer

If you find that your computer is running slowly or that frequent program glitches are hurting your productivity, you can often solve these problems by resetting your PC's system files. The Reset this PC feature reinstalls a fresh copy of Windows. It also saves the documents, images, and other files in your user account, some of your settings, and any Windows apps that you have installed. However, Reset this PC does *not* save any other PC settings (which are reverted to their defaults) or any desktop programs that you installed.

Refresh Your Computer

1 In the taskbar's Search box, type **reset**.

2 Click **Reset this PC**.

The Settings app runs and selects the Recovery tab.

3 Under Reset this PC, click **Get started**.

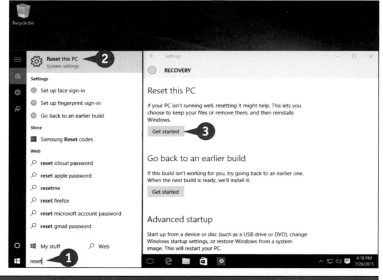

Reset this PC asks you to choose a reset option.

4 Click **Keep my files**.

Reset this PC displays a list of software you will need to reinstall.

5 Click **Next**.

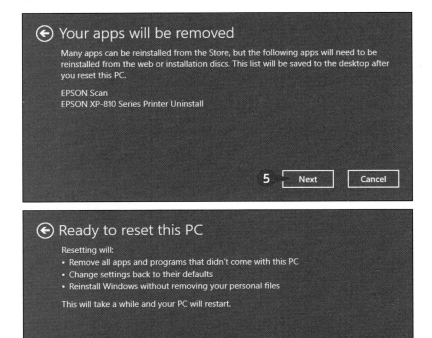

Your apps will be removed

Many apps can be reinstalled from the Store, but the following apps will need to be reinstalled from the web or installation discs. This list will be saved to the desktop after you reset this PC.

EPSON Scan
EPSON XP-810 Series Printer Uninstall

5 — Next Cancel

6 Click **Reset**.

Reset this PC reboots the computer and refreshes the system files.

Ready to reset this PC

Resetting will:
- Remove all apps and programs that didn't come with this PC
- Change settings back to their defaults
- Reinstall Windows without removing your personal files

This will take a while and your PC will restart.

6 — Reset Cancel

TIP

How do I refresh my computer if I cannot start Windows?

1 Insert your installation disc or recovery drive and then restart your computer.

2 Boot to the disk or drive.

3 In the Windows Setup dialog box, click **Next**.

4 Click **Repair your computer**.

5 Click **Troubleshoot**.

6 Click **Reset this PC**.

7 Click **Keep my files**.

8 Click your user account, type your account password, and then click **Continue**.

9 Click **Reset**.

Create a Recovery Drive

You can make it easier to troubleshoot and recover from computer problems by creating a USB recovery drive. If a problem prevents you from booting your computer, then you must boot using some other drive. If you have your Windows installation media, you can boot using that drive. If you do not have the installation media, you can still recover if you have created a recovery drive. This is a USB flash drive that contains the Windows recovery environment, which enables you to refresh or reset your PC, recover a system image, and more.

Create a Recovery Drive

1 Insert the USB flash drive you want to use.

2 In the taskbar's Search box, type **recovery drive**.

3 Click **Create a recovery drive**.

The User Account Control dialog box appears.

4 Click **Yes**.

Note: If you are using a standard account, enter your PC's administrator credentials to continue.

The Recovery Drive Wizard appears.

5 Click **Next**.

The Recovery Drive Wizard prompts you to choose the USB flash drive.

6 Click the drive if it is not selected already.

7 Click **Next**.

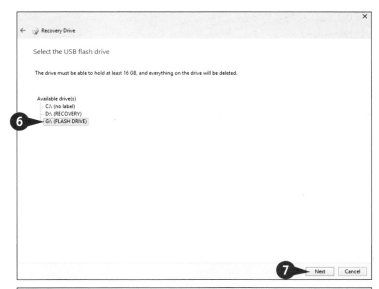

The Recovery Drive Wizard warns you that all the data on the drive will be deleted.

8 Click **Create**.

The wizard formats the drive and copies the recovery tools and data.

9 Click **Finish** (not shown).

TIPS

Can I use any USB flash drive as a recovery drive?
No. The drive must have a capacity of at least 16GB. Windows erases all data on the drive, so make sure the flash drive does not contain any files you want to keep.

How can I make sure the recovery drive works properly?
You should test the drive by booting your PC to the drive. Insert the recovery drive and then restart your PC. How you boot to the drive depends on your system. Some PCs display a menu of boot devices; select the USB drive from that menu. In other cases, a message tells you to press a key.

Keep a History of Your Files

There may be times when backing up a file just by making a copy is not good enough. For example, if you make frequent changes to a file, you might want to copy not only the current version, but also the versions from an hour ago, a day ago, a week ago, and so on. In Windows, these previous versions of a file are called its *file history*, and you can save this data for all your documents by activating a feature called File History.

Keep a History of Your Files

Set the File History Drive

1 Connect an external drive to your PC.

Note: The drive should have enough capacity to hold your files, so an external hard drive is probably best.

Note: If you see a notification, click it, click **Configure this drive for backup**, and then skip steps **3** and **4**.

2 In the taskbar's Search box, type **history**.

3 Click **File History**.

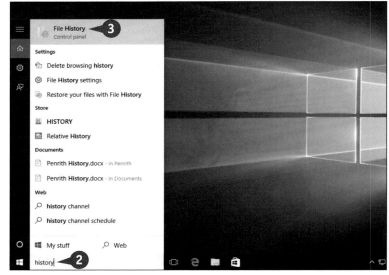

The File History screen appears.

A If Windows detects an external hard drive, it displays the drive here.

Note: If this is the correct drive, you can skip steps **4** to **6**.

4 Click **Select drive**.

The Select Drive window appears.

5 Click the drive you want to use.

6 Click **OK**.

Activate File History

1 Click **Turn on**.

Windows activates File History and begins saving copies of your files to the external drive.

Is it okay to disconnect the external hard drive temporarily?
Yes. However, if you need to remove the external drive temporarily (for example, if you need to use the port for another device), you should turn off File History before disconnecting the external drive. Follow steps **2** and **3** to open the File History screen and then click **Turn off**. When you are ready to resume saving your files, follow steps **1** to **3** to reconnect the drive and open the File History screen, and then click **Turn on**.

Restore a File from Your History

If you improperly edit, accidentally delete, or corrupt a file through a system crash, in many cases you can restore a previous version of the file. Why would you want to revert to a previous version of a file? One reason is that you might improperly edit the file by deleting or changing important data. In some cases, you may be able to restore that data by going back to a previous version of the file. Another reason is that the file might become corrupted if the program or Windows crashes. You can get a working version of the file back by restoring a previous version.

Restore a File from Your History

1 In the taskbar's Search box, type **restore files**.

2 Click **Restore your files with File History**.

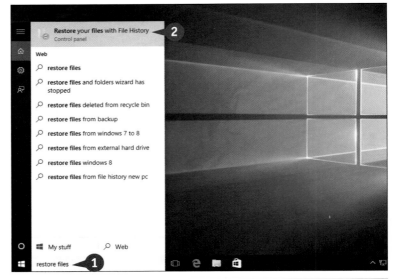

The Home - File History window appears.

3 Double-click the library or folder that contains the file you want to restore.

4 Open the folder that contains the file.

5 Click **Previous Version** (◄|) until you open the version of the folder you want to use.

6 Click the file you want to restore.

7 Click **Restore to Original Location** (⟳).

If the original folder has a file with the same name, File History asks what you want to do.

8 Select an option:

Click **Replace the file in the destination** to overwrite the existing file with the previous version.

Click **Skip this file** to do nothing.

Click **Compare info for both files** to decide which file you prefer to keep.

Windows restores the previous version.

TIPS

Can I restore a folder?
Yes, because Windows also keeps track of previous versions of folders, which is useful if an entire folder becomes corrupted. Follow steps **1** to **5**, click the folder you want to restore, and then click **Restore to Original Location** (⟳).

What should I do if I am not sure about replacing an existing file with a previous version?
Click **Compare info for both files** in the Replace or Skip Files dialog box. In the File Conflict dialog box, click the check box beside both versions (☐ changes to ☑) and then click **Continue**. This leaves the existing file as is and restores the previous version with (2) appended to the name.

Check Your Hard Drive for Errors

To keep your system running smoothly, you should periodically check your hard drive for errors and fix any errors that come up. Because hard drive errors can cause files to become corrupted, which may prevent you from running a program or opening a document, you can use the Check Disk program to look for and fix hard drive errors.

Check Your Hard Drive for Errors

1 Click **File Explorer**.

File Explorer appears.

2 Click **This PC**.

3 Click the hard drive that you want to check.

4 Click the **Computer** tab.

5 Click **Properties**.

The hard drive's Properties dialog box appears.

6 Click the **Tools** tab.

7 Click **Check**.

Ⓐ If Windows tells you that the drive has no errors, you can click **Cancel** and skip the rest of these steps.

❽ Otherwise, click **Scan drive**.

Windows checks the hard drive.

❾ When the check is complete, click **Close**.

Note: If Check Disk finds any errors, follow the instructions the program provides.

What is a "bad sector"?

A *sector* is a small storage location on your hard drive. When Windows saves a file on the drive, it divides the file into pieces and stores each piece in a separate sector. A bad sector is one that, through physical damage or some other cause, can no longer be used to reliably store data.

How often should I check for hard drive errors?

You should perform the basic hard drive check about once a week. Perform the more thorough bad sector check once a month. Note that the bad sector check can take several hours, depending on the size of the drive, so perform this check only when you will not need your computer for a while.

Check Your Devices for Errors

To help ensure that your system is operating smoothly and efficiently, you should periodically check for errors associated with the devices attached to your computer. Device errors usually mean either that you cannot work with a device entirely, or that the device behaves erratically or unexpectedly. You can use the Windows Devices and Printers feature to check your installed devices for errors. You can also use Devices and Printers to troubleshoot your problem devices, and in most cases Windows will be able to fix the problem automatically.

Check Your Devices for Errors

Check for Devices with Errors

1 In the taskbar's Search box, type **view devices**.

2 Click **Devices and Printers**.

The Devices and Printers window appears.

3 Examine the device icons for errors.

A Windows indicates devices with errors using this icon (⚠).

Begin Device Troubleshooting

1 Click a device that has an error.

2 Click **Troubleshoot**.

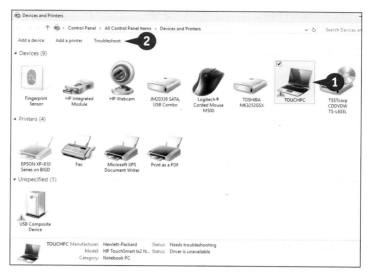

The Devices and Printers troubleshooting wizard appears and displays the first fix.

3 Click **Apply this fix**.

Devices and Printers applies the fix. If this does not solve the problem, Devices and Printers displays the next fix.

B If you are certain this fix is not the solution, click **Skip this fix** instead.

4 Repeat step **3** until the problem is resolved.

TIPS

What is a device driver?

It is a small program that Windows uses to communicate with a device. Many hardware problems are the result of either not having a device driver installed, or having an incorrect driver installed. Most devices come with discs that have the correct device driver, so you should insert that disc when troubleshooting. You can also obtain the latest device driver from the manufacturer's website.

What if Devices and Printers cannot solve the problem?

In this case, you need to either return the device to the manufacturer for repair or replacement, or take it to a local computer shop for fixing.

Defragment Your Hard Drive on a Schedule

You can make Windows, and your programs, run faster, and your documents open more quickly, by defragmenting your hard drive on a regular schedule. File fragmentation means that a file is stored on your hard drive in multiple pieces instead of as a single piece. This slows performance because it means that when Windows tries to open such a file, it must make several stops to collect the various pieces. A lot of fragmented files can slow down even the fastest hard drive. Defragmenting improves performance by bringing all those pieces together, making finding and opening each file faster.

Defragment Your Hard Drive on a Schedule

1 In the taskbar's Search box, type **defragment**.

2 Click **Defragment and Optimize Drives**.

The Optimize Drives window appears.

3 Click **Change settings**.

The Optimization Schedule dialog box appears.

④ Click **Run on a schedule (recommended)** (☐ changes to ☑).

⑤ Click the **Frequency** ⌄ and then click the frequency with which you want to defragment (Daily, Weekly, or Monthly).

⑥ Click **OK**.

Ⓐ The new schedule appears here.

Ⓑ If you want to defragment your drives now, click **Optimize**.

⑦ Click **Close**.

How often should I defragment my hard drive?
This depends on how often you use your computer. If you use your computer every day, you should defragment your hard drive weekly. If you use your computer only occasionally, you should defragment your hard drive monthly.

How long does defragmenting my hard drive take?
It depends on the size of the hard drive, the amount of data on it, and the extent of the defragmentation. Budget at least 15 minutes for the defragmenting, and know that it could take more than an hour.

Create a System Restore Point

If your computer crashes or becomes unstable after you install a program or a new device, the System Restore feature in Windows can fix things by restoring the system to its previous state. To ensure this works, you need to set restore points before you install programs and devices on your computer.

Windows automatically creates system restore points as follows: every week (called a *system checkpoint*); before installing an update; and before installing certain programs (such as Microsoft Office) and devices. These are useful, but it pays to err on the side of caution and create your own restore points more often.

Create a System Restore Point

1 In the taskbar's Search box, type **restore**.

2 Click **Create a restore point**.

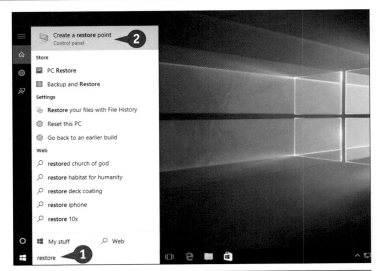

The System Properties dialog box appears.

Ⓐ The System Protection tab is already displayed.

3 Click **Create**.

The Create a Restore Point
dialog box appears.

4 Type a description for your
restore point.

5 Click **Create**.

System Restore creates the
restore point.

Windows tells you the restore
point was created successfully.

6 Click **Close**.

7 Click **OK** to close the System
Properties dialog box.

TIPS

On my system, the Create button is disabled. How can I fix that?
If the Create button is disabled, it means that System Restore is turned off. To turn it on, click your hard drive in the Available Drives list, click **Configure**, click **Turn on system protection** (○ changes to ◉), and then click **OK**.

When should I create a restore point?
To be safe, you should create a restore point before you install any software, whether you purchased the program at a store or downloaded it from the Internet. You should also create a restore point before you add any new hardware devices to your system.

Apply a System Restore Point

If your computer becomes unstable or behaves erratically after you install a program or device, you can often fix the problem by applying the restore point you created before making the change. If after you install a program or device you notice problems with your system, the easiest solution is to uninstall the item. If that does not work, then your next step is to revert to an earlier restore point. Windows reverts your computer to the configuration it had when you created the restore point, which should solve the problem.

Apply a System Restore Point

1 In the taskbar's Search box, type **restore**.

2 Click **Create a restore point**.

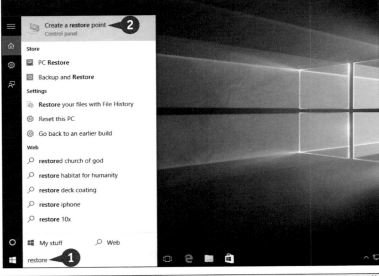

3 Click **System Restore**.

4 Click **Next**.

System Restore prompts you to choose a restore point.

5 Click the restore point you want to apply.

6 Click **Next**.

The Confirm Your Restore Point window appears.

7 Click **Finish**.

System Restore asks you to confirm that you want to restore your system.

8 Click **Yes**.

System Restore applies the restore point and then restarts Windows.

TIPS

Will I lose any of my recent work when I apply a restore point?
No, the restore point reverts only your computer's configuration back to the earlier time. Any work you performed in the interim — documents you created, emails you received, web page favorites you saved, and so on — is not affected when you apply the restore point. However, if you installed any programs after the restore point, you must reinstall those programs.

If applying the restore point makes things worse, can I reverse it?
Yes. Follow steps **1** to **4** to display the list of available restore points on your computer. Click the **Restore Operation** restore point and then follow steps **6** to **8**.

Index

A

accessing
- app features, 36–37
- Lock command, 297
- OneDrive online, 243
- shared documents/folders, 267

account password, 286

accounts, 113, 254–255

activating file history, 317

adding
- apps to Lock screen, 32–33
- captions to images in OneNote, 225
- desktops, 46
- event reminders, 121
- events to calendars, 118–119
- extra fields to contacts in People app, 110–111
- file attachments to email messages, 78–79
- files to OneDrive, 242–243
- Google account to People app, 100–101
- iCloud account to People app, 102–103
- images to notebook pages, 224–225
- Microsoft Exchange account to Mail app, 73
- pages to OneNote notebooks, 220
- photo effects, 170–171
- recipes to Food & Drink app, 149
- sections to OneNote notebooks, 221
- text notes in OneNote, 222–223
- titles to images in OneNote, 225
- typed notes, 65
- web pages to Favorites Bar, 62

adjusting
- audio levels for CDs, 189
- contact's photos in People app, 109
- copy quality, 193
- Cortana settings, 131
- file view, 234
- homegroup password, 263
- Lock screen background, 30–31
- picture passwords, 293
- playlists, 199
- screen brightness, 282
- section color schemes in OneNote notebooks, 221
- speed of slide shows, 167
- startup page, 58–59
- text font in documents, 208–209
- user account password, 258–259
- user account pictures, 256–257
- volume, 40, 201

Alarm & Clock app, 152–153

albums
- art for, 189
- buying, 195
- viewing images by, 165

All Apps list, starting apps from, 17

all-day events, 119

annotating web pages, 64

applying
- Selective Focus effect, 171
- styles to messages, 77
- system restore points, 328–329
- Vignette effect, 171

apps. *See also specific apps*
- accessing features, 36–37
- adding to Lock screen, 32–33
- checking weather forecast, 136–137
- configuring Cortana Voice Assistant, 130–131
- displaying locations on maps, 132–133
- finding recipes, 148–149
- following favorite teams, 146–147
- getting directions to locations, 134–135
- installing, 14–15
- looking up health information, 150–151
- pinning
 - to Start menu, 26–27
 - to taskbar, 38–39
- searching your PC, 128–129
- setting alarms, 152–153
- shutting down with gestures, 275
- starting, 16–17
- stopping notifications from, 303
- switching between running, 18–19
- tracking stocks, 144–145
- uninstalling, 22–23
- updating, 20–21
- writing notes, 154–155

arranging windows, 19

assigning photos to contacts in People app, 108–109

attachments, adding to email messages, 78–79

audio levels, changing for CDs, 189

automatic image repair, 168

Automatic install, compared with Custom install, 23

automating updates, 21

Index

Index